Island Statesmen

Island Statesmen

Small Nations, Big Diplomacy

Selma Aarvik

Mindful Pages

Published in 2026

ISBN: 9789376556823 (PB)
ISBN: 9789376559596 (eBook)

Published by

Mindful Pages
Imprint of Alpha Editions LLC
312 W. 2nd St #1834
Casper, WY 82601, USA

Content

Introduction

On 14 December 2015, in the cavernous General Assembly Hall of the United Nations in New York, a woman representing a Pacific island state with fewer than 120,000 citizens pressed the microphone button at her desk. The room hummed with translation headsets and the faint rustle of paper. Outside, snow softened the city. Inside, her voice carried for barely three minutes. There were no theatrics, no raised volume. Yet by the following summer, a clause she had insisted upon—quietly, repeatedly—had reshaped how vulnerability was recognised in the allocation of climate finance under the Paris Agreement. Cargo insurers noticed. Development banks adjusted templates. The speech itself dissolved into the archive, but its effects travelled, like a tide that keeps moving long after the moon has passed its highest point.

How does something so small move something so vast? That question sits at the centre of a paradox that modern diplomacy prefers not to examine too closely. The architecture of international politics is built around size: territory measured in square kilometres, populations counted in tens of millions, budgets with enough zeroes to blur the eye. And yet, again and again, states that would barely register on a world map find ways to bend rules, stall decisions, or tilt outcomes that appear, at first glance, far beyond their reach. The contrast is not merely rhetorical. According to the World Bank's 2022 classification, more than thirty sovereign states have populations under half a million; collectively, they account for a minute fraction of global GDP. Still, their fingerprints appear on shipping conventions, debt frameworks, climate texts and security arrangements that shape the lives of billions.

The smell of strong coffee lingers in many of these moments. It hangs in small mission offices near First Avenue before dawn, in borrowed meeting rooms in Bonn or Nairobi, in hotel corridors where negotiations continue after the formal sessions end. Influence, for small nations, is rarely exercised under bright lights. It is applied obliquely, with patience, through words chosen to survive drafts and redrafts, through timing that turns procedural trivia into strategic openings. This book follows the island statesmen and women whose names seldom headline communiqués, but whose decisions, careers and habits of mind have redirected flows of goods, money and norms. Their biographies read like footnotes; their effects do not.

The conventional story of power remains stubborn. It traces a straight line from land to labour, from factories to force, from military capacity to diplomatic weight. In that story, small states appear as dependants or irritants, buffered by geography or absorbed into the shadow of larger neighbours. Yet that lens struggles to explain why, in September 2021, a Caribbean country with a single deep-water port was able to delay consensus at the International Maritime Organization long enough to secure stricter fuel standards for vessels transiting its waters, or why, in October 2018, a coalition led by Indian Ocean islands forced a recalibration of how "loss and damage" was framed at a climate conference in Katowice. These were not accidents. They were the product of craft.

Craft is the through-line here. It is visible in how agendas are read like tide tables, in how legal language is tested for stress points, in how moral claims are translated into procedural footholds. Consider the negotiations over exclusive economic zones in the western Pacific during the late 2000s. For larger states, maritime boundaries were one file among many. For microstates whose land barely rose above sea level, the surrounding ocean represented food security, revenue and sovereignty. By commissioning meticulous hydrographic surveys and registering claims early with the United Nations Division for Ocean Affairs, these governments transformed abstract geography into enforceable jurisdiction. The act was technical, almost dull. Its implications were not: control over fisheries worth hundreds of millions of dollars annually, as estimated by the Food and Agriculture Organization in 2019.

Still, there are limits. Smallness does not confer automatic virtue or success. In May 2020, as the pandemic collapsed tourism and dried up remittances, several island economies found that moral authority carried little weight with private creditors. Bondholders, dispersed and unsentimental, demanded payment. Appeals to vulnerability stalled. The asymmetry was real, and painful. Any honest account must hold these failures alongside the quieter victories. Influence, for small states, is contingent and perishable. It depends on preparation, credibility and the willingness to accept trade-offs that larger actors can often avoid.

The people at the centre of these stories matter disproportionately. In a foreign service of fifty officers, an ambassador's temperament shapes an entire portfolio. Long tenures allow for institutional memory that larger bureaucracies often diffuse. In February 2017, in Geneva, a trade negotiator from a landlocked enclave state was able to recall, from personal experience, how a similar clause had been neutralised a decade earlier. That recollection altered the room's dynamics. Careers in such settings are not interchangeable. They are accumulations of trust, fatigue, intuition and stubbornness. The biographies traced here are not celebrations of heroism; they are studies in how individual agency intersects with structural constraint.

Climate diplomacy provides perhaps the clearest illustration of how lived experience becomes political capital. For low-lying islands, climate change is not a scenario modelled in reports but a sequence of storms, saline wells and eroding graves. When representatives speak of degrees and baselines, they do so with images of flooded schools in mind. That translation—from the local to the universal—has reshaped negotiations. In Paris in 2015, and again in Glasgow in November 2021, island envoys insisted on language that linked emissions trajectories to the survival of cultures, not just ecosystems. The move was deliberate. By reframing the issue as one of loss rather than cost, they altered the moral geometry of the room. Funds followed language, imperfectly but measurably, as new financing windows were debated in subsequent years.

Law, too, becomes a strategic asset when force is unavailable. Maritime arbitration cases brought by small states rarely attract headlines, yet their outcomes reverberate. In July 2014, when an arbitral tribunal clarified safety obligations in a disputed strait in Southeast Asia, the immediate parties were modest coastal nations. The beneficiaries included shipping companies and insurers worldwide, who adjusted routes and premiums accordingly. The lawyers involved operated far from gunboats. Their tools were precedent, patience and an intimate understanding of procedure. Such cases show how, under certain conditions, courts can substitute for cannons.

Money complicates the picture. Debt has a different texture in economies with narrow tax bases and limited diversification. Servicing obligations can crowd out the mundane investments that make resilience possible: reinforcing a seawall, upgrading a port crane, retaining trained nurses. Negotiations with creditors become exercises in narrative as much as arithmetic. In March 2019, a finance minister from a southern African island state walked into a meeting in London with a slide deck that avoided ratios and instead traced, photograph by photograph, how a cyclone had undone years of progress. The restructuring that followed did not erase the burden, but it stretched time enough to breathe. It also demonstrated how economic diplomacy, in small states, collapses the distinction between domestic survival and foreign policy.

Soft power, often treated as an indulgence of the affluent, acquires sharper edges in tourism-dependent economies. Reputation is revenue. When beaches are polluted or visitors mistreated, the effects are immediate. Governments learn to speak to airlines, film producers and journalists with a clarity born of necessity. In June 2016, a Mediterranean island used the prospect of reputational damage to compel a multinational cruise operator to invest in waste management upgrades at its main port. The negotiation hinged less on regulation than on image. Culture, in these instances, is not decoration. It is currency.

Beyond formal channels, diasporas operate as dispersed embassies. Concentrated in certain cities and sectors, they relay information, mobilise attention and sometimes lobby with a fluency unavailable to official missions. Their influence is uneven and occasionally unruly. Coordination is hard. Yet in October 2020, when a community organisation in a North American capital organised briefings for legislators on sea-level rise, the talking points echoed those used by the home country's ambassador weeks earlier. The amplification was not accidental. It was planned, and it mattered.

The multilateral system itself rewards those who read it closely. Calendars, provisional agendas and review cycles create seams where pressure can be applied. In April 2018, a diplomat from a Pacific microstate noticed that an obscure committee report was scheduled for discussion when larger delegations would be thinly staffed. By preparing early and rallying a small caucus, she turned a footnote into a platform for ocean literacy that later surfaced in higher-profile resolutions. Gains of this sort are incremental. Their accumulation is the point.

Regional blocs and issue-based alliances magnify voice but carry risks. Alignment with larger sponsors can deliver protection or access, but it can also mute dissent. When a long-standing ally shifts priorities, small states feel the tremor first. Hedging—diversifying partners, cultivating alternative forums—becomes a survival skill. Success stories here are rarely dramatic. They are marked by avoided crises and quietly improved terms.

Gender threads through these dynamics in ways both constraining and enabling. In small foreign services, visibility cuts sharply. Women who lead negotiations on security or finance navigate expectations that oscillate between scepticism and symbolism. Their successes recalibrate norms. When a foreign minister insists that junior women be included in every delegation, the policy change is immediate and personal. It also alters the future talent pool.

And yet, the motif returns: the tide. Influence advances and retreats. There are moments when size overwhelms skill, when external shocks flatten even the most carefully built positions. Recognising this does not diminish the achievements described here. It sharpens them. The craft of asymmetric diplomacy is not about winning every battle. It is about choosing where to stand so that, when the water moves, it carries something with it.

The world that small states navigate is tightening. Climate impacts accelerate. Debt markets harden. Multilateral norms fray under geopolitical strain. Decisions made in distant capitals reverberate quickly along fragile coastlines. Against this backdrop, the question is not whether small nations can match the power of giants. It is whether they can continue to translate their particular vulnerabilities and assets into forms of influence that endure. The answer is not settled. It is being tested, clause by clause, case by case, often over coffee in rooms too small for history books.

Chapter 1
Why Small States Matter

On a humid afternoon in July 2019, delegates filed into a conference room in Apia, Samoa, for what was meant to be a routine regional trade meeting. Ceiling fans pushed warm air across the room. Coffee cups clinked. At the edge of the table sat the representative of a state whose entire population would barely fill a mid-sized football stadium. When the chair called for consensus on a technical amendment to a draft agreement, the larger economies nodded and prepared to move on. The small state did not. Its delegate asked for time, then raised a narrow procedural objection grounded in the text's own rules. The room stalled. By evening, the amendment had been rewritten to protect shipping preferences critical to that country's sole port. Size had not disappeared. It had simply ceased to decide the outcome.

Moments like this rarely enter the public imagination. They lack spectacle. There are no aircraft carriers or emergency summits. And yet they reveal something fundamental about how contemporary power actually works. The assumption that influence scales neatly with territory or population is deeply ingrained, but increasingly unreliable. A country with one airport and one harbour lives with a different calculus of risk and opportunity than a continental giant with dozens of both. That difference does not vanish at negotiating tables; it sharpens. Constraints compress choice, but they also focus attention. When options are few, strategy becomes explicit.

The term "small state" itself resists tidy definition. Some scholars draw lines at population counts or gross domestic product; others distinguish microstates from merely small ones. Island states, enclaves surrounded by larger neighbours, and city-sized polities all fall somewhere along this spectrum. What unites them is not a number but a condition: limited room for manoeuvre in land, labour and revenue, coupled with acute exposure to external decisions. A single cyclone, a change in shipping insurance, a new banking rule drafted thousands of miles away can reorder national priorities overnight. Smallness, in this sense, is not a badge but a lived reality that shapes how politics is practised.

Consider the contrast between a large continental power and a tiny island economy. The former can absorb shocks by rerouting trade through alternative ports, shifting fiscal resources across regions, or drawing on vast domestic markets. The latter often relies on one deep-water harbour, one international airport, and a handful of export earners. If that port closes, the state holds its breath. If that airport loses a route, the budget feels it immediately. This fragility is often mistaken for weakness. It is more accurately a form of concentration. What is essential becomes unmistakable, and diplomacy follows those fault lines.

Classical thinking about power has long privileged accumulation. From early geopolitical theorists to twentieth-century realists, influence has been mapped onto landmass, industrial output and military capability. In such frameworks, small states appear as footnotes: buffer zones between rivals, clients to be protected or pressured, prizes to be traded. Agency flows downhill. Initiative belongs to those with scale. This view has explanatory force when tanks cross borders or when industrial mobilisation determines victory. It falters in conference rooms, courtrooms and committee hearings, where outcomes hinge on wording, timing and legitimacy.

Repeatedly, small states have demonstrated the capacity to initiate rather than merely react. In regional trade talks, they have blocked consensus by insisting on unanimity clauses written into founding charters. In environmental negotiations, they have reframed technical debates as moral tests, altering the reputational stakes for larger players. These actions do not overturn hierarchies. They complicate them. They reveal that power is not only about imposing preferences, but about shaping the field on which preferences are expressed.

To see this clearly requires a shift in question. Instead of asking who is strongest, it is more revealing to ask who can delay a decision, who can unlock a stalled process, who can redefine what counts as success or failure at a given moment. This is the logic of leverage. It is situational, relational and often transient. Agenda control can matter more than voting weight. Legal instruments can substitute for force. Media narratives can impose costs that balance sheets alone cannot measure. A state that controls a narrow shipping channel, a key transhipment port or a crucial data cable landing point may exert influence disproportionate to its size, not by threatening others, but by structuring their choices.

Shipping offers a concrete illustration. Global trade depends on predictable routes and safe harbours. When a small coastal state tightens environmental standards for vessels entering its main port, it is not merely regulating locally; it is signalling norms that ripple through insurance markets and fleet management decisions. Population size does not determine the effect. Geography, law and credibility do. Similar dynamics play out in finance, where the consent of a handful of vulnerable borrowers can shape the terms of collective debt initiatives, or in climate diplomacy, where the lived experience of risk lends urgency to abstract models.

Still, leverage is not a magic key. It operates within constraints that are real and sometimes unforgiving. A small state that overplays its hand may find partners drifting away. One that relies too heavily on a single tactic risks being sidelined when circumstances change. The spectrum of smallness includes variation not only in capacity but in resilience. Some polities have diversified economies and deep diplomatic benches; others depend on a few overstretched officials juggling multiple portfolios. Recognising this diversity is essential. It prevents romanticism and grounds analysis in practice.

This is where individual biographies become indispensable. In large states, policy outcomes are often the product of layers of bureaucracy that blur personal contribution. In small states, the line between person and policy is thinner. An ambassador's relationships, a minister's negotiating style, a legal adviser's persistence can leave discernible marks on treaties and institutions. Careers unfold in public view, within societies where reputations travel fast and mistakes linger. Studying these lives is not an exercise in personality worship. It is a way of tracing how structural limits are navigated day by day.

Biographies also reveal the craft that statistics conceal. They show how envoys learn to read rooms, how they decide when to speak and when to wait, how they translate domestic anxieties into language that travels. They expose the quiet labour behind moments that, in hindsight, appear inevitable. When a small state blocks a consensus or inserts a clause that later proves decisive, the act rests on months or years of preparation by individuals whose names rarely appear in headlines. Their stories anchor abstract concepts in human experience.

The present moment sharpens the relevance of this inquiry. Global challenges increasingly disregard borders while being mediated through institutions that still privilege sovereign consent. Climate change, financial volatility, pandemics and technological shifts impose pressures that fall unevenly, often hardest on those with the least buffer. At the same time, the multilateral system shows signs of strain. Rules are contested. Trust is uneven. In such an environment, the ability of small states to exercise informed, strategic influence becomes more than a curiosity. It becomes a test of whether international cooperation can accommodate vulnerability without reducing it to charity.

There is a temptation to treat small states as moral barometers rather than strategic actors, valuing their voices for what they symbolise rather than what they achieve. This, too, is a distortion. Moral authority matters, but it gains traction only when paired with procedural skill and institutional memory. The diplomats and ministers encountered in this chapter are neither saints nor victims. They are practitioners, working within tight margins, making trade-offs that larger states often evade. Their successes illuminate possibilities; their failures warn against complacency.

As the chapter unfolds, the reader moves from definitions that resist rigidity to scenes that test inherited assumptions. The spectrum of smallness comes into focus not as a taxonomy but as a set of conditions that invite particular responses. Traditional views of power are examined not to dismiss them, but to expose their blind spots. Leverage emerges not as a slogan, but as an observable pattern in how decisions are shaped. And through carefully chosen lives, the abstraction of "the small state" acquires texture: accents, habits, anxieties, and the steady accumulation of experience.

The stakes are quiet but high. If influence is possible without mass, then the architecture of global politics is more flexible than it appears. If it is not, then vulnerability risks hardening into irrelevance. The answer lies not in theory alone, but in practice, in rooms like the one in Apia where a raised hand can pause a process and alter its direction. Understanding why such moments occur, and how they are made, is the work of this chapter. It opens a door onto a world where size still matters, but never in the way it seems.

Defining microstates and small nations

On 1 January 1995, as the World Trade Organization came into force in Geneva, the delegation of Malta consisted of fewer people than the security staff at the entrance. The island's entire land area measures just over 300 square kilometres; its population then stood at roughly 370,000. One harbour. One international airport. One customs authority tasked with translating a new global trade regime into domestic law. The asymmetry was stark. Yet Malta acceded as a full member, with the same formal rights as economies hundreds of times its size. The room was quiet. The rules were not. Scale did not disappear; it took a different shape. Boundaries matter here.

The difficulty begins with names. "Microstate" suggests minuteness without context, a label that risks condescension. "Small nation" sounds gentler but remains vague. Both are often treated as categories with thresholds, as if sovereignty changes character at a particular population count or income level. That instinct is misleading. Smallness is not a switch but a gradient. It is experienced as a series of pressures that accumulate: limited territory constrains infrastructure; small populations thin labour markets; narrow tax bases tighten budgets. Each pressure narrows margins. Together, they shape how a polity moves.

A single gate changes behaviour.

Island states, landlocked enclaves, and city-sized polities share this condition despite their differences. Geography fixes certain facts early. An island's perimeter is water; an enclave's borders are someone else's. A city-state's hinterland is diplomatic rather than physical. These realities impose constraints that are immediately legible to officials and citizens alike. When there is one port, it is inspected relentlessly. When there is one airport, its runway length becomes a national concern. Fiscal room for manoeuvre follows similar lines. With few sectors and volatile revenues, budgets respond quickly to shocks. Decision-makers feel the weight of each choice because there are fewer buffers to absorb error.

This is not an argument for rigid definitions. Population thresholds—100,000 here, one million there—offer convenience but little insight. A state of 80,000 with a diversified services economy and a stable legal regime may enjoy more effective capacity than a state of 800,000 dependent on a single commodity. Smallness operates as a spectrum, shaped by exposure and concentration rather than by headcount alone. What matters is not how many people live within a border, but how many options the state can realistically exercise when circumstances shift.

Observation clarifies this. Large continental powers typically distribute risk. They can relocate production, reroute logistics, and adjust policy incrementally. Small states concentrate risk. The same port handles food imports, fuel deliveries, and export earnings. The same ministry drafts climate policy, negotiates loans, and staffs international missions. This concentration has a name: dependency density. It explains why policy horizons shorten and why external decisions reverberate loudly at home. It also explains why attentiveness to rules, schedules, and procedures becomes a survival skill.

The traditional literature on power rarely pauses here. From classical geopolitics to mid-twentieth-century realism, influence is treated as a function of accumulation. Territory offers resources; population offers labour and soldiers; industry offers output; military capacity offers coercion. In this frame, small states appear as derivatives. They are buffers between rivals, pawns in balance-of-power games, or clients reliant on protection. Agency flows from the centre outward. Initiative belongs to those who can impose costs unilaterally.

The empirical record complicates that story. Small states repeatedly initiate outcomes disproportionate to their material weight. In March 2016, at a meeting of the Southern African Development Community in Gaborone, a landlocked country with a GDP under USD 20 billion delayed approval of a transport protocol by invoking a unanimity rule embedded in the organisation's founding treaty. The delay forced revisions to protect its rail access to coastal ports. The behaviour was observable: a procedural objection, sustained over hours. The concept is clear: rule-based veto. The consequence was tangible: altered text with economic effects.

Such cases do not refute the importance of size; they show where size is less decisive than expected. Influence in these settings hinges on position within institutional machinery. Agenda placement, drafting rights, and timing can outweigh raw capacity. This is particularly true in forums where consensus norms prevail and where legitimacy matters. A small state that knows the rules intimately can slow a process, force clarification, or reframe debate. The effect resembles hydraulics more than force: pressure applied at a narrow point moves a larger body.

A second example illustrates the geographic dimension. Singapore is often excluded from discussions of microstates because of its wealth, yet its physical constraints are instructive. With no natural resources and limited land, it invested heavily in becoming indispensable to maritime trade. By 2020, the Port of Singapore handled over 37 million twenty-foot equivalent units, according to the Maritime and Port Authority of Singapore. Control of transhipment capacity translated into regulatory voice. Standards adopted locally influenced regional shipping practices. The observation is concrete: throughput. The explanation lies in chokepoints. The consequence is influence without hinterland.

Still, there are limits to this pattern. Not all small states can convert constraint into leverage. Some lack administrative capacity; others face political instability that erodes credibility. In June 2022, a Pacific island government announced an ambitious maritime surveillance initiative, only to see it stall amid budget shortfalls and staff turnover. Geography offered potential leverage; institutions could not sustain it. This limitation matters. It cautions against romanticising smallness as inherently empowering. Spectrum cuts both ways.

Understanding microstates and small nations, then, requires attention to behaviour rather than labels. How many simultaneous negotiations can a foreign ministry sustain? How quickly can legislation be amended? How exposed is the economy to a single external decision? These questions translate abstraction into metrics. They also reveal why individual officials loom larger. When a ministry has ten diplomats rather than a thousand, each person carries institutional memory. Absence is felt. Continuity becomes precious.

The motif of the single gate returns here. A state with one port inspects it obsessively; a state with one vote in a committee guards it carefully. Both acts stem from the same logic: when points of access are few, their management becomes strategic. This logic underpins why small states invest heavily in legal literacy and procedural competence.

Law offers predictability where force does not. Process offers leverage where numbers fall short.

City-sized polities sharpen this dynamic further. Enclaves such as Monaco or San Marino operate within dense webs of agreements that substitute for territory. Their sovereignty is thin but precise. Decisions are calibrated to avoid friction with neighbours while preserving autonomy in niches—finance, culture, dispute resolution. The observable behaviour is selectivity. The concept is specialisation. The consequence is survival with influence in narrow domains.

Fiscal room for manoeuvre remains the hardest constraint. Limited revenues compress policy space. Debt accumulates quickly after shocks. Choices become stark. A finance minister deciding between servicing bonds and repairing a seawall does not deliberate in the abstract. The trade-off is immediate and political. Small states respond by seeking predictability: multi-year financing, rules-based aid, insurance mechanisms. These preferences carry into diplomacy, shaping positions on climate finance and debt relief. What appears as moral argument often originates in budget spreadsheets.

The continental contrast clarifies the point. A large state can afford redundancy. Multiple ports compete; airports absorb delays; regions cross-subsidise. Failure is localised. For a microstate, failure is systemic. This difference does not disappear in negotiations. It informs tone, urgency, and persistence. When a small-state delegate insists on a clause, it is often because there is no fallback. The insistence is not rhetorical; it is structural.

And yet, the spectrum allows movement. Some small states climb toward resilience through diversification and institutional investment. Others slide toward vulnerability through mismanagement or external shocks. The category remains fluid. What endures is the pattern of concentrated exposure. Recognising this pattern helps explain why small states behave as they do without reducing them to caricature.

The sharpened test, then, is practical. When confronted with a new rule, shock, or opportunity, how many doors does the state have? How many gates can it open or close? The answer determines strategy. It also determines whether smallness becomes a constraint endured or a condition worked. The distinction is neither sentimental nor fixed. It is made, repeatedly, at the single gate where global systems meet local limits.

Traditional views of power and size

In September 1945, as delegates gathered in San Francisco to finalise the Charter of the United Nations, the arithmetic of power was written into the room. Five states secured permanent seats on the Security Council. The rest did not. The logic was explicit and unapologetic: those with the largest populations, the widest territories, the deepest industrial bases and the most formidable militaries would shoulder responsibility for order. Power would follow mass. Smaller states would be protected, represented, or managed. The building itself reinforced the message. Flags lined the entrance, equal in height, but everyone understood where decisions would settle. Weight counted. That assumption has travelled far.

It remains the default grammar of international politics. Open a textbook, skim a strategy paper, listen to a briefing on "great power competition," and the same variables recur: land, people, production, force. These are not trivial measures. They explain much about war, deterrence and coercion. They also frame how small states are imagined: as dependencies reliant on patronage, as buffer zones separating rivals, or as bargaining chips traded to stabilise larger balances. The model is coherent. It is also incomplete.

Size looks decisive. Often it is.

The thesis here is narrow but consequential. Classical size-based theories of power systematically miss forms of initiative that do not rely on accumulation. They undercount the influence exercised through rules, procedures, and timing, and they misread the behaviour of small states as passive or reactive when it is frequently strategic. This is not a rejection of material power. It is an argument about where it ceases to explain outcomes, particularly in institutional settings where consent, legitimacy and process matter.

Observation makes this visible. Large states tend to act through scale: mobilising resources, projecting force, absorbing costs. Small states act through position: locating points where modest actions produce outsized effects. The name for this difference is not weakness but orientation. One approach overwhelms. The other redirects. When analysis focuses only on the former, the latter appears anomalous or invisible.

The classical canon offers reasons. Early geopolitical thinkers such as Halford Mackinder treated landmass as destiny. Control the "heartland," control the world. Later realists translated this spatial logic into variables of population and industrial capacity. Military strength followed. The behaviour predicted by these models fits many historical cases, particularly those involving conquest or deterrence. It fits less well in committee rooms, arbitration panels, and trade negotiations, where outcomes hinge on unanimity rules, drafting authority, and reputational costs.

A concrete case sharpens the point. On 12 July 2019, during negotiations of the Pacific Agreement on Closer Economic Relations Plus in Apia, Samoa, a country with a population under 200,000 withheld consent over a technical annex governing rules of origin. Its GDP was negligible compared to Australia or New Zealand, the agreement's anchors. Yet the rules required consensus. The delegation cited concerns about domestic processing thresholds that would disadvantage its sole export industry. The behaviour was observable: refusal to nod. The concept is procedural veto.

The consequence was renegotiated text. No tanks moved. No sanctions loomed. Size did not decide.

Traditional frameworks struggle with such moments because they treat institutions as reflections of underlying power rather than arenas with their own physics. In reality, institutions often flatten differences temporarily. One vote equals one vote. One objection delays all. These mechanics are not accidents; they are design choices meant to legitimise outcomes. Small states learn them early. Mastery of process becomes a form of capacity. When analysis ignores this, it mistakes skill for luck.

The same blindness appears in how dependency is understood. Small states are often described as dependent on larger ones for security or markets. The observation is accurate. The name given to it—dependency—implies asymmetry without agency. It suggests a one-way flow of influence. In practice, dependency frequently creates leverage points. A larger state reliant on basing rights, transit access, or diplomatic support inherits vulnerabilities of its own. The smaller partner can exploit these carefully, not by confrontation, but by conditional cooperation.

Consider Iceland during the Cold War. With no standing army and a population under 200,000, it relied on the United States for defence through NATO. Dependency seemed total. Yet Iceland repeatedly used its strategic location astride North Atlantic sea lanes to extract concessions, threatening to withdraw basing rights unless fishing limits were respected. The Cod Wars of the 1950s to

1970s were not wars in any conventional sense, but they altered maritime boundaries in Iceland's favour. The observation is clear: threats without force. The explanation lies in chokepoints. The consequence was expanded jurisdiction over fisheries vital to the economy.

These cases expose a flaw in size-centric thinking: it conflates capacity with effect. Capacity refers to what a state can mobilise internally. Effect refers to what its actions produce externally. The two correlate imperfectly. A large state may possess immense capacity yet struggle to translate it into effect in settings where legitimacy, consensus, or law constrain action. A small state may lack capacity yet achieve effect by positioning itself where marginal moves matter.

A second example, more contemporary, comes from trade. In December 2013, at the Ninth WTO Ministerial Conference in Bali, consensus on a trade facilitation agreement hinged on acceptance by all members. A group of developing countries, including several microstates, signalled reservations over implementation costs. Their economies were tiny within the WTO's aggregate figures. Their behaviour was decisive. The delay forced accommodations on technical assistance and timelines. The metric was simple: unanimity. The abstraction is bargaining power. The outcome was altered obligations.

Critics respond with a limitation that deserves attention. These moments, they argue, occur only because larger states permit them. When stakes rise high enough, power asserts itself. Military force bypasses procedure. Sanctions overwhelm vetoes. There is truth here. Small-state initiative operates within bounds. It cannot compel outcomes in existential conflicts. When major security interests are engaged, the room narrows sharply.

Acknowledging this does not dissolve the argument; it refines it. The claim is not that size is irrelevant, but that its relevance varies by context. In arenas governed by rules that require consent or value legitimacy, small states possess tools that size-centric models discount. When conflicts shift into arenas of coercion, those tools lose purchase. The choice for analysts is not between models, but between domains. Applying the wrong lens produces error.

The motif that binds these observations is friction. Classical power assumes smooth surfaces: force applied produces movement proportional to magnitude. Institutional politics introduces friction points where movement stalls unless specific conditions are met. Small states study these points closely. They know where decisions catch. They learn which phrases trigger review, which committees control flow, which calendars create leverage. This attention to friction explains behaviours that otherwise seem obstructive or pedantic.

Observable behaviours make this tangible. Small-state delegations arrive early. They read footnotes. They track who chairs which meeting. They invest in legal advice rather than public relations. These choices are not cultural quirks; they are adaptations. When votes are equal but voices are not, precision compensates for volume. When resources are thin, continuity substitutes for breadth.

Traditional views also misread motivation. Small states are often portrayed as risk-averse, clinging to rules because they fear exposure. The observation is partial. Rules offer shelter, but they also offer opportunity. A state that cannot impose outcomes may still shape them by defining acceptable conduct. Law becomes a multiplier. Procedure becomes a shield and a lever. This duality escapes models that treat norms as epiphenomena of power rather than as instruments.

Yet friction cuts both ways. Overreliance on procedural tactics can breed reputational costs. A state that blocks too often may find itself isolated. In April 2021, a regional organisation in the Caribbean amended its decision-making rules after repeated delays attributed to a single member's objections. The change reduced that member's leverage. The limitation is clear: rules can be rewritten. Initiative invites response.

This dynamic suggests a trade-off rather than a triumph. Small states must decide when to exercise friction and when to yield. Each intervention draws attention. Each delay tests patience. The calculus is delicate. It requires judgement rather than doctrine. Classical size-based theories offer little guidance here because they abstract away from process.

Returning to the opening image of San Francisco in 1945, the Charter did not eliminate small states' agency; it channelled it. One vote in the General Assembly remains one vote. One objection in certain forums still stalls progress. These design features coexist with great power privileges. The architecture is hybrid. Analysing it with a single variable obscures how influence actually moves.

The sharpened choice for the reader is analytical. When assessing an outcome, does one look first to mass or to mechanics? Does one ask who is largest, or who was positioned to apply friction at the decisive moment? The answer determines whether small-state initiative appears anomalous or intelligible. The test is empirical. Trace the rule invoked, the procedure used, the calendar exploited. Where those elements decide outcomes, size alone cannot explain power.

Rethinking leverage in global forums

On 23 March 2021, a container ship named *Ever Given* ran aground in the Suez Canal, wedged diagonally across a channel barely wider than itself. For six days, global trade slowed to a crawl. Lloyd's List estimated that roughly USD 9.6 billion in cargo was delayed each day as vessels queued at either end. Egypt's population exceeded 100 million; the canal authority itself employed a fraction of that. Yet for one week, the ability to move goods between Asia and Europe hinged on decisions taken in Ismailia, not Beijing or Brussels. The lesson was blunt. Strength did not determine the moment. Position did.

Leverage begins where force pauses.

The central claim of this book takes shape here. Power, as commonly described, measures capacity. Leverage measures effect. It asks not who commands the largest resources, but who can alter the path of a decision at the point where movement is constrained. In global forums governed by rules, schedules and reputations, leverage often accrues to those who can stall, unlock or reframe choices at critical junctures. This shift in question—from magnitude to mechanics—reorients how influence is identified and exercised, particularly by small states.

Observation makes the distinction concrete. Strong actors push. Leveraged actors position. The former rely on accumulation; the latter on placement. This is not a semantic preference. It reflects different logics of action. In a multilateral negotiation, the ability to introduce an agenda item, to insist on a review clause, or to draw public attention to an unresolved risk can outweigh the capacity to threaten retaliation. The concept that names this pattern is leverage. Its consequences include delayed votes, amended texts and altered expectations.

Agenda control offers the clearest illustration. Meetings appear neutral; they are not. What is scheduled, when it is scheduled, and in which sequence issues are addressed shape outcomes before arguments begin. Small-state delegations invest disproportionate energy here. They read provisional agendas line by line. They track reporting cycles. They notice when a technical item is placed late on a Friday, when attendance thins. The behaviour is observable:

early submission of proposals, quiet objections to sequencing. The explanation lies in path dependence. Once an issue is framed and timetabled, reversing it becomes costly. The consequence is influence exercised before confrontation.

Legal tools operate similarly. Courts, tribunals and arbitration panels convert asymmetry into procedure. A state that cannot coerce can still litigate. The act of filing a case freezes certain behaviours, attracts scrutiny, and forces responses within defined timelines. In July 2014, the Permanent Court of Arbitration's ruling in a maritime dispute clarified safety and environmental obligations in contested waters. The claimant was a small coastal state. The respondent possessed far greater military capacity. The immediate effect was not compliance, but a shift in the legal and diplomatic terrain. Insurance assessments changed. Third parties adjusted conduct. The leverage lay not in enforcement, but in definition.

Media narratives add a third layer. Global forums are not sealed rooms. Statements leak. Drafts circulate. Images travel. Small states cultivate visibility strategically, not continuously. They choose moments when attention amplifies stakes. A press conference timed to coincide with a stalled negotiation can impose reputational costs on larger actors sensitive to public perception. The behaviour is timed disclosure. The explanation is reputational risk. The consequence is altered bargaining posture.

These mechanisms share a motif: the hinge. Leverage operates at hinges—points where systems turn on small inputs. Shipping channels, unanimity rules, reporting deadlines, and headlines all function as hinges. Control the hinge, and size recedes. Miss it, and capacity dominates.

A short maritime example distils the argument. The Bosphorus Strait, governed by the Montreux Convention of 1936, channels traffic between the Black Sea and the Mediterranean. Turkey's population and economy are significant, but its leverage here does not derive from size alone. It derives from custodianship of a passage that handles tens of thousands of transits annually. In March 2022, amid heightened security concerns, Turkey invoked provisions of the Convention to restrict certain naval movements. The decision shaped naval deployments by far larger powers. The metric was traffic volume. The abstraction is chokepoint authority. The outcome was strategic restraint imposed without force.

Leverage does not require drama. More often, it manifests in accumulation of small adjustments. Consider how small island states have influenced climate negotiations. By insisting that references to "loss and damage" remain distinct from adaptation, they preserved conceptual space that later supported financing discussions. The act was textual. The effect was fiscal. The behaviour involved bracketed language and repeated interventions. The explanation lies in semantic persistence. The consequence emerged years later in funding debates.

Yet leverage has limits that must be acknowledged to avoid myth-making. It depends on rules remaining intact and audiences remaining attentive. When rules are bypassed or when attention shifts, hinges can seize. In February 2022, several multilateral processes stalled as geopolitical conflict drew focus elsewhere. Small states' agenda items slipped. Their leverage diminished not because their skill eroded, but because the forum's relevance waned. This limitation matters. Leverage is situational, not absolute.

Reconciling this limitation sharpens rather than weakens the concept. It suggests that leverage must be renewed. It is not a stockpile; it is a practice. States that rely on it invest in institutional memory, legal expertise and communications capacity. They monitor when forums matter and when they do not. They redeploy attention accordingly. The behaviour is adaptation. The explanation is forum volatility. The consequence is resilience across settings.

Another constraint arises from overuse. A state that stalls too often risks isolation. Reputational capital can be depleted. In October 2018, a small European state faced pushback in a regional council after repeated procedural objections slowed budget approvals. Other members amended rules to limit vetoes. The hinge moved. The lesson is clear. Leverage invites countermeasures. Its exercise requires calibration.

What distinguishes leverage from mere obstruction is intent. Stalling without a pathway forward exhausts goodwill. Stalling to unlock a reframed option can shift outcomes. This distinction appears in observable choices: whether objections are paired with alternatives, whether legal actions are accompanied by negotiation, whether media engagement leaves room for compromise. Leverage works best when it opens doors rather than slams them.

Agenda control, law and narrative interact. A case filed gains traction when reported. A story resonates when anchored in text. A scheduled debate becomes decisive when linked to legal consequences. Small states that succeed in global forums rarely rely on a single tool. They braid them. The braid is thin but strong.

The hinge motif returns here. Each strand aligns at a turning point. Miss the alignment, and nothing moves. Achieve it, and motion follows with little force. This is why population size often misleads analysts. It measures potential, not placement.

The practical implication is analytical discipline. When assessing influence, ask where decisions hinge. Who controls access to that hinge? Who understands its tolerances? The answers often point away from the largest actors. They point to those who arrived early, read carefully, and waited.

The trade-off at the close is stark. Invest in mass, or invest in mechanics. Large states do both by default. Small states must choose. The testable next step is empirical: trace an outcome backwards. Identify the hinge. Measure who touched it. Where leverage explains movement better than size, the traditional map of power needs redrawing.

How this book uses biographies

On a cold morning in February 2014, in a narrow conference room at the International Tribunal for the Law of the Sea in Hamburg, the lead counsel for a small West African state adjusted his papers and waited. Outside, the harbour cranes stood still. Inside, the judges took their seats. The case concerned maritime boundaries with far-reaching economic implications, yet the delegation behind him could fit around a single table. The counsel, appointed after years in a modest foreign ministry, knew every comma in the brief. When the ruling came months later, it clarified jurisdiction over waters far larger than the country's land territory. The decision is cited in textbooks. The man who argued it is barely known. The scale of effect and the scale of the actor diverged sharply. That divergence is the point.

This book chooses to begin not with models, but with people. The decision is deliberate. In small states, the distance between individual action and collective outcome is unusually short. A single envoy can carry an entire portfolio. A minister's judgement can redirect a negotiation. Where bureaucracies are thin, personalities leave traces. Ignoring that fact produces elegant theories and inaccurate explanations.

Biography, used carefully, offers a way to see how leverage is actually made.

The thesis is straightforward. Abstract models of diplomacy describe constraints well but often misrepresent agency. They treat states as unitary actors responding predictably to incentives. In large systems, the simplification can hold. In small ones, it distorts. Outcomes there frequently hinge on the habits, skills and endurance of particular people operating within tight structural limits. Short biographies, anchored in verifiable moments, reveal how craft interacts with constraint. They show what leverage looks like in practice, not as a concept but as a sequence of decisions.

Observation grounds this claim. In a foreign service with fewer than fifty officers, posting choices matter intensely. An ambassador may serve a decade in the same capital, accumulating trust and informal access that no organisational chart captures. The behaviour is visible: repeated meetings, handwritten notes, early arrivals. The name for this accumulation is relational capital. The consequence is continuity that outlasts electoral cycles and policy fashions.

Consider Dame Meg Taylor of Papua New Guinea, appointed Secretary-General of the Pacific Islands Forum in 2014 and based in Suva, Fiji. Her tenure coincided with heightened regional coordination on climate and fisheries. Taylor's background—as a lawyer with deep regional ties—shaped how the Forum spoke and acted. She insisted on legal clarity in communiqués and invested time in aligning diverse island positions before major global meetings. The outcome was not rhetorical unity alone, but coordinated interventions that larger partners had to address. The observation is her sustained presence. The explanation lies in personal credibility. The consequence was a stronger regional voice.

Biography also illuminates trade-offs invisible in structural analysis. Small-state diplomats rarely specialise narrowly. One week they brief ministers on debt, the next they draft environmental language, then they host visiting delegations. This breadth imposes cognitive load and rewards adaptability. Careers become exercises in triage. What to pursue. What to drop. Models assume capacity; lives reveal scarcity.

A second example comes from the Caribbean. Sir Ronald Sanders of Antigua and Barbuda has represented his country in Washington and at the Organization of American States for decades. His long tenure allowed him to navigate shifting administrations and maintain focus on issues vital to small island economies, including correspondent banking access. When U.S. regulators tightened rules in the mid-2010s, threatening to sever banking links, Sanders leveraged personal relationships to keep the issue on agendas otherwise dominated by security concerns. The metric was time: years of engagement. The abstraction is persistence. The outcome was sustained attention to a problem that might otherwise have been dismissed as marginal.

Such cases demonstrate why biography matters. They show how leverage is built through repetition and memory. They also reveal costs. Long-serving figures risk becoming gatekeepers. Renewal can stall. When a respected envoy retires, institutional knowledge may evaporate. The limitation is real. Biography can explain success and fragility simultaneously.

This book does not present lives as isolated narratives. Each biography is paired with a pattern. An ambassador's career opens onto maritime law. A finance minister's trajectory illuminates debt diplomacy. A climate negotiator's path reveals how vulnerability is translated into text. The individual is the entry point, not the endpoint. Through them, broader dynamics come into focus.

The motif binding these portraits is the craft bench. Diplomacy, in small states, resembles skilled manual work more than abstract strategy. Tools are few. Materials are constrained. Results depend on technique. Watching the craftsperson at work reveals choices that diagrams conceal. Which clause to sand down. Which joint to reinforce. When to step back.

Observable behaviours bring this craft into view. A seasoned envoy keeps annotated drafts from past negotiations. A minister rehearses interventions aloud to test tone. A legal adviser consults academic networks late at night to confirm precedent. These acts are mundane. They are also decisive. Biography captures them because it follows time and habit.

Abstract models struggle here because they prioritise equilibrium over process. They predict where systems settle, not how they get there. In small-state diplomacy, the journey often determines the destination. A misjudged remark can close doors for years. A well-timed question can reopen them. Lives record these inflection points.

There is, however, a risk in biographical focus: over-attribution. It is tempting to credit individuals for outcomes shaped by context. This book resists that temptation by treating biography as a lens, not a cause. Structural constraints remain decisive. A gifted envoy cannot conjure capacity where none exists. They can, however, deploy what exists more effectively. Reconciling agency and structure requires attention to both.

An example of limitation clarifies this balance. In 2020, a small island state appointed a charismatic new ambassador to lead negotiations on climate finance. Despite skill and visibility, progress stalled as donor priorities shifted amid a global crisis. The individual performed well. The structure constrained outcomes. Biography explains effort; context explains result. Both matter.

The decision to use short biographies rather than extended life histories reflects respect for the reader's time and for evidence. Each portrait is selective, anchored in episodes that illuminate a broader point. The aim is not completeness, but relevance. Details earn their place by clarifying how leverage operates under constraint.

These biographies also serve continuity. Across chapters, patterns recur. The same individual may appear briefly in different contexts, linking climate talks to financial negotiations, regional blocs to global forums. Careers in small states rarely follow single tracks. Their intersections reveal how issues connect. A maritime lawyer becomes a climate negotiator. A finance minister becomes a foreign policy actor. Biography traces these crossings naturally.

The craft bench motif returns here. Each chapter places a different tool on the bench: law, agenda control, narrative, coalition-building. The biographies show hands using them. Without the hands, the tools remain inert. Without the tools, the hands falter. The pairing matters.

For readers accustomed to models and metrics, this approach may feel indirect. It asks patience. The reward is accuracy. Seeing how a clause survives, how a meeting is delayed, how an alliance holds reveals more about power than aggregate figures alone. It also restores human responsibility. Decisions are made by people, under pressure, with incomplete information.

The sharpened choice at the close is methodological. To understand influence in small states, one can study systems from above or lives from within. This book chooses the latter, not to reject theory, but to test it against practice. The testable next step is simple. When an outcome surprises, trace the individuals involved. Follow their paths. At the craft bench, leverage becomes visible.

Chapter 2
Climate Diplomacy from Vulnerable Shores

Just before dawn on 6 November 2022, in Sharm el-Sheikh, an ambassador from a low-lying Pacific island sat alone in a hotel room overlooking the Red Sea. The air-conditioning hummed. On the desk lay two documents: a draft speech for the opening week of COP27 and a set of photographs sent overnight from home. They showed a village shoreline after a king tide, water lapping at the steps of a church, breadfruit trees standing in brackish pools. The speech spoke of targets, pathways, and commitments. The photographs spoke of loss already incurred. She moved a paragraph down the page, crossed out a sentence, and replaced it with another that linked the fate of those trees to decisions being made thousands of miles away that very week. Outside, the conference centre lights flickered on. The negotiation day began long before the plenary hall filled.

For island states on the front line of climate change, the distinction between present and future has collapsed. Sea-level rise is measured not in projections but in centimetres marked on seawalls. Storms are recalled by name, date, and cost. Fisheries shift. Wells turn saline. When their representatives speak in global forums, they do so not as messengers of abstract risk but as witnesses to ongoing disruption. This proximity to impact has altered the moral geometry of climate diplomacy. Vulnerability, once treated as a plea for sympathy, has become a claim to standing.

Climate politics is often narrated as a contest between emitters and reducers, between development and restraint. That framing obscures another axis that matters profoundly: exposure. Small island states contribute a negligible share of global greenhouse gas emissions—well under one per cent collectively, according to the Intergovernmental Panel on Climate Change's Sixth Assessment Report in 2021—yet they absorb disproportionate harm. The asymmetry is stark and persistent. It is also politically potent when articulated with precision.

The power of this articulation does not lie in melodrama. It lies in translation. Island diplomats have learned to translate lived experience into language that survives contact with negotiating text. Survival appears not as a metaphor but as a legal question. Stewardship of the oceans is framed not as romance but as responsibility. When ambassadors speak of reefs, they are speaking of food security. When they speak of relocation, they are speaking of sovereignty. The themes recur because the realities recur.

At climate conferences, preparation often begins far from the negotiating floor. An envoy may spend a morning in a coastal community meeting elders who recall when the shoreline sat twenty metres further out. In the afternoon, she may brief a regional caucus on draft language circulated overnight. In the evening, she rewrites her intervention to ensure that a local story aligns with a clause under discussion. This movement between scales—village to plenary—defines front-line climate diplomacy. It is not performative. It is strategic.

Vulnerability, when framed carefully, becomes leverage. The shift is subtle but decisive. Rather than asking for indulgence, small states pose a test of fairness. If climate change is a collective problem, then those least responsible and most affected carry a particular claim. This claim reshapes negotiating space by reframing what counts as reasonable. Emissions decisions taken elsewhere are linked explicitly to immediate threats to homes, reefs, and fisheries. The causal chain is shortened. Delay acquires faces.

A telling example emerged during the negotiations leading to the Glasgow Climate Pact in November 2021. A small delegation from the Indian Ocean pressed for stronger language on sea-level rise, insisting that it be treated not merely as a long-term concern but as a current driver of displacement. The initial draft softened the issue. Through repeated interventions, coordinated with other vulnerable states, the delegation succeeded in inserting language that acknowledged present impacts. The change did not transform global policy overnight. It did, however, alter the baseline for subsequent discussions. Text matters. Once words enter a decision, they travel.

This reframing extends beyond mitigation into the contested terrain of finance. Climate finance debates are often technical, dense with acronyms and accounting rules. Small states have steered these debates toward predictability and responsibility. The argument is consistent: adaptation cannot depend on discretionary generosity; it requires reliable support anchored in obligation. This is not charity. It is risk management.

Loss and damage crystallises this tension. For decades, the concept sat uneasily at the margins of climate negotiations, resisted by those wary of liability. Island states persisted. They argued that when territory is lost, when freshwater is contaminated, when cultural sites disappear, the issue is not adaptation failure but irreparable harm. The language shifted slowly. At COP27, the agreement to establish funding arrangements for loss and damage marked a turning point, however incomplete. The path there was paved by coalitions of small states that refused to let the issue recede, even when progress seemed unlikely.

Coalition-building is essential here. No microstate advances these claims alone. Regional groupings such as the Alliance of Small Island States coordinate positions, share intelligence, and divide labour. One delegation may focus on finance, another on legal framing, a third on media engagement. The choreography is deliberate. It reflects an understanding that moral authority gains traction when paired with procedural discipline.

The envoys who carry this work often share distinctive profiles. Many are trained lawyers, comfortable with text and precedent. Many maintain close ties to their communities, returning home frequently, absorbing the stories that animate their interventions. Many serve long tenures, building relationships across conferences that span years. Their authority grows not from titles alone but from consistency. They are recognised faces in rooms where attendance rotates rapidly.

Consider a negotiator from a Caribbean microstate who began her career as an environmental impact assessor. By the time she led her country's delegation to a major climate summit in Madrid in 2019, she could recite, from memory, how changes in reef health affected fish catches in specific bays. In plenary, she used those details sparingly, aligning them with legal arguments about state responsibility. Delegates listened. The combination of specificity and restraint commanded attention.

Climate diplomacy from vulnerable shores also involves risk. The moral appeal can be dismissed as emotional. The repetition can fatigue audiences. There is a danger of being typecast as victims rather than partners. Savvy envoys counter this by coupling vulnerability with proposals. They speak of renewable energy potential, of blue economy strategies, of regional knowledge hubs. Stewardship becomes forward-looking. Agency reasserts itself.

The chapter ahead traces these dynamics through lives and moments. It examines how island states have learned to navigate the long arc of climate negotiations, from early pleas for recognition to sophisticated bargaining over finance and responsibility. It follows envoys as they move between community meetings and global summits, carrying with them not only data but obligation.

The stakes are not confined to islands. As climate impacts intensify, the questions these states raise—about fairness, responsibility, and the meaning of loss—will confront all societies. Island diplomats operate as early interlocutors in a conversation the world cannot avoid. Their shores are vulnerable. Their arguments are not.

What unfolds next is neither a catalogue of suffering nor a manual of advocacy. It is an examination of how proximity to harm reshapes diplomacy, how lived experience becomes political currency, and how small states have carved space in one of the most complex negotiations of our time. The tide is rising. So is the craft of those who have learned to speak from its edge.

Front line island climate diplomacy

On 8 November 2013, Typhoon Haiyan made landfall in Tacloban, Philippines, with winds exceeding 300 kilometres per hour. By the time the storm surge receded, more than 6,000 people were dead, entire neighbourhoods had been flattened, and the shoreline had shifted inland. One year later, at the opening of the twentieth Conference of the Parties to the UN Framework Convention on Climate Change in Lima, the Philippine negotiator Yeb Saño stood before delegates and spoke of bodies found tangled in trees and of a country "still reeling". The room fell silent. This was not a forecast. It was an account. The datum was devastation already counted.

For low-lying and storm-exposed island states, climate change does not arrive as a scenario. It arrives as an invoice. Homes are rebuilt twice. Wells are replaced. Coastlines retreat metre by metre. The waterline moves. What distinguishes front line island diplomacy is not emotional intensity but temporal clarity. Risk is not deferred. It is present tense. That clarity has reshaped how these states speak and, more importantly, how they are heard.

The central claim here is precise. Lived vulnerability, when translated with discipline, has become a source of moral and political authority in climate negotiations. This authority does not rest on spectacle or sentiment. It rests on proximity. Island diplomats occupy a position where the consequences of inaction are observable within a single electoral cycle. That immediacy alters the burden of argument. It forces a shift from abstract optimisation to concrete responsibility.

Observation grounds the claim. In speeches by island representatives, certain themes recur with notable consistency. Survival appears early, not as hyperbole but as a legal fact tied to habitability and statehood. Stewardship follows closely, particularly of the oceans that surround and sustain these polities. The behaviour is patterned: references to reefs, fisheries, and coastal protection appear alongside calls for emissions cuts. The name for this pairing is custodial authority. The consequence is a reframing of islands from victims to guardians.

This reframing matters because climate negotiations are crowded with competing claims. Large emitters emphasise development needs. Vulnerable states emphasise exposure. Island diplomats have learned to connect the two without collapsing them. When they speak of stewardship, they are not asserting moral superiority; they are asserting stakes. The ocean is not a backdrop. It is infrastructure. Damage there reverberates through food systems, employment, and culture.

The waterline motif captures this dynamic. On islands, the waterline is watched daily. Children learn where it sat when their grandparents were young. Engineers mark it against seawalls. Elders measure it against graves. This attentiveness becomes political. When envoys speak of sea-level rise, they often do so in centimetres already observed, not projections alone. According to the Intergovernmental Panel on Climate Change's Sixth Assessment Report in 2021, global mean sea level rose by about 20 centimetres between 1901 and 2018, with acceleration in recent decades. For islands, that number has names and addresses.

A second, quieter observation concerns preparation. Island climate diplomacy is meticulous. Delegations are small, but briefs are dense. Envoys arrive with photographs, tide charts, and local testimonies vetted for accuracy. The behaviour is evidentiary discipline. The explanation lies in credibility. Claims grounded in lived experience invite scrutiny; they must withstand it. The consequence is authority earned through restraint.

A brief vignette brings this into focus. On the eve of COP26 in Glasgow in October 2021, an ambassador from a Micronesian state sat in a borrowed office near the River Clyde, rehearsing remarks for a high-level segment. Her draft ran to two pages. She cut it to one. She removed a metaphor and replaced it with a statistic from her national meteorological service documenting the frequency of king tides since 2005. She checked the wording against the latest draft decision text to ensure alignment. The final speech lasted under two minutes. It landed because it was exact.

This craft reflects a deeper strategic choice. Island states rarely win arguments by volume. They win by forcing alignment between evidence and principle. Climate vulnerability becomes leverage when framed as a test of fairness that others must answer. If global action is delayed, who bears the cost? If adaptation funding is discretionary, who absorbs the risk? These questions reposition island states from petitioners to examiners.

Historical examples illustrate the point. In December 2009, at COP15 in Copenhagen, small island states pushed for recognition of the 1.5°C temperature threshold, arguing that 2°C represented existential risk for them. The push failed formally at the time. The observation was resistance. The name was marginalisation. The consequence was persistence. Over the following decade, the threshold re-emerged, supported by accumulating science and repeated advocacy. By the time of the Paris Agreement in 2015, it was embedded in the text as an aspirational goal. Persistence altered baselines.

Another example lies in the evolution of ocean-focused climate initiatives. Island states insisted that ocean health be recognised within climate frameworks long before it gained mainstream traction. Through side events, joint declarations, and targeted interventions, they linked acidification, warming, and sea-level rise to climate mitigation. The behaviour was agenda expansion. The explanation was existential linkage. The consequence was the gradual integration of ocean considerations into climate discourse, including the launch of initiatives such as the Ocean Pathway Partnership in 2019.

The authority derived from vulnerability, however, is not unlimited. There is a credible limitation that island diplomats acknowledge privately. Repetition risks fatigue. Audiences may harden. Appeals grounded solely in suffering can be discounted as predictable. The danger is being typecast as tragic rather than strategic. Reconciling this requires balance.

Successful envoys manage the balance by coupling vulnerability with stewardship and solution-building. They speak not only of loss but of agency: renewable energy transitions, marine protected areas, and regional early-warning systems. The message shifts from "we are harmed" to "we are acting; join us". The waterline returns here, not only as threat but as measure of responsibility. If islands can adapt within tight constraints, larger states can do more.

Observable decisions reinforce this approach. Island states often overperform on climate ambition relative to their size, submitting nationally determined contributions that commit to rapid transitions. The metric is percentage reduction. The abstraction is credibility. The consequence is moral symmetry: demands on others are paired with action at home.

There is also a legal dimension. For some island states, climate change raises questions of territory and sovereignty. What happens if land becomes uninhabitable? Can maritime zones persist? These questions surface cautiously in negotiations, often framed as requests for clarification rather than confrontation. The behaviour is anticipatory lawmaking. The explanation lies in risk management. The consequence is early shaping of norms that may matter profoundly in future disputes.

The front line experience also alters diplomatic tone. Island envoys tend to avoid apocalyptic rhetoric. They prefer plain description. Storm names are cited. Dates are fixed. Repair costs are enumerated. According to the World Bank's 2018 estimates, climate-related disasters cost small island developing states an average of 2–3 per cent of GDP annually, with spikes far higher after major events. Such figures appear in speeches not to shock but to anchor claims.

The waterline motif appears again in coalition work. Island states often describe themselves as "canaries", but the more accurate image is that of sentinels posted at the edge. They detect changes early. They report back. This role confers responsibility as much as vulnerability. It also explains why their interventions often look ahead, warning of impacts that others will face later. The consequence is a temporal advantage in agenda-setting.

As negotiations move deeper into finance and implementation, front line diplomacy faces new tests. Moral authority must translate into institutional change. Predictable funding, insurance mechanisms, and legal recognition of loss require technical engagement. Island envoys step into these debates with the same discipline they bring to speeches. Vulnerability opens doors; competence keeps them open.

The section closes on a choice that island diplomats confront repeatedly. How hard to press. How much to concede. When to invoke lived experience directly, and when to let text carry the weight. The trade-off is constant. Press too softly, and urgency dissipates. Press too hard, and partners withdraw. Navigating this line is the essence of front line climate diplomacy.

The waterline continues to move. So does the practice of those who speak from it. Their authority does not derive from size or force. It derives from standing where consequences arrive first, and from learning how to turn that position into words that travel.

Using climate risk as leverage

On the night of 12 December 2015, as negotiations over the Paris Agreement stretched past their scheduled close in Le

Bourget, a small island delegation huddled around a marked-up draft. Outside the plenary hall, delegates from major economies debated percentages and timelines. Inside the huddle, the island negotiators focused on a single phrase concerning sea-level rise. The draft referred to it as a "long-term concern". The delegation objected. By the time the gavel fell the following afternoon, the language had shifted to recognise "the urgent threat of sea-level rise to the existence of small island developing states". No emissions targets changed that night. The text did. And text, in climate diplomacy, accumulates force.

Climate risk becomes leverage when it ceases to be a warning and becomes a test.

The thesis is exact. Climate vulnerability translates into bargaining power not through sympathy, but through reframing. When island states frame climate change as a question of global fairness—linking decisions made elsewhere to immediate, identifiable losses at home—they alter the terms of negotiation. Emissions are no longer abstract units to be optimised. They are causal agents connected to disappearing land, collapsing fisheries, and the erosion of culture. This reframing constrains what others can plausibly argue without reputational cost.

Observation clarifies the mechanism. In formal negotiations, island envoys rarely speak first about carbon budgets. They begin with consequences. The behaviour is consistent: homes inundated during king tides, reefs bleached beyond recovery, fishing grounds rendered unpredictable. The name for this move is causal compression. The explanation lies in accountability. Shortening the causal chain between action and harm limits rhetorical escape routes. The consequence is a narrowing of acceptable positions.

This narrowing does not rely on exaggeration. It relies on verifiable facts. According to the Intergovernmental Panel on Climate Change's Sixth Assessment Report in 2021, even under low-emissions scenarios, sea levels will continue to rise for centuries, with impacts intensifying for low-lying coasts. Island negotiators translate this into present stakes. They cite the frequency of flooding events, the cost of relocating infrastructure, the loss of arable land. Metrics replace metaphor.

The fairness frame sharpens further when responsibility enters the discussion. Island states contribute negligibly to global emissions, yet they face some of the highest per capita climate costs. The World Bank estimated in 2018 that climate-related disasters could cost small island developing states up to 9 per cent of GDP annually under certain scenarios. When envoys present such figures, they do not plead incapacity. They assert imbalance. The bargaining implication is clear: those who benefit most from emissions-intensive growth carry a differentiated responsibility to address its harms.

Reframing climate change as loss rather than risk intensifies this effect. Risk implies probability and choice. Loss implies fact. When negotiators speak of territory that may become uninhabitable, they are not speculating. They are inventorying what is at stake. Territory is not merely land; it anchors maritime zones, citizenship rights, and political identity. Culture follows territory. Graves, languages, and rituals are place-bound. Their disappearance is irreversible. Introducing these dimensions expands the negotiating space by introducing values that resist monetisation.

A concrete example illustrates how this reframing operates in practice. During preparatory negotiations for COP26 in 2021, a small coalition of island states objected to draft language that treated sea-level rise primarily as an adaptation challenge. They argued that for some states, adaptation could not prevent loss of territory. Through coordinated interventions across working groups, they pressed for recognition of "irreversible loss". The behaviour was textual persistence. The explanation was legal foresight. The consequence was language that acknowledged limits to adaptation, strengthening the conceptual foundation for subsequent loss and damage discussions.

The lever here is subtle. Text does not compel action. It legitimises claims. Once loss is acknowledged, funding debates change character. They move from voluntary assistance to questions of obligation. Island states have exploited this shift carefully, avoiding explicit liability language while insisting on responsibility. The result is a discursive corridor within which new mechanisms can be proposed.

This approach also reshapes how emissions reductions are discussed. By linking emissions elsewhere to immediate harm at home, island envoys undermine narratives that treat mitigation as a trade-off between present costs and future benefits. The costs are present. The benefits are preventative. This inversion challenges incrementalism. It places pressure on timelines and ambition. The bargaining effect is incremental but cumulative.

The motif that binds these strategies is the ledger. Climate diplomacy, as practised by island states, resembles accounting more than prophecy. Losses are logged. Responsibilities are apportioned. Entries accumulate. The ledger does not close quickly. It does, however, make denial harder. Each new entry references those before it, building a record that others must confront.

Media engagement amplifies this ledger when deployed sparingly. Island delegations often choose moments when negotiations stall to draw attention to specific losses. Images of flooded homes or eroded coastlines appear alongside citations from draft texts. The behaviour is selective disclosure. The explanation is reputational leverage. The consequence is external scrutiny that alters internal dynamics within negotiating blocs.

A second named example underscores the point. In November 2018, during COP24 in Katowice, Poland, representatives from the Marshall Islands and allied states highlighted recent flooding events in Majuro while negotiating transparency rules. They linked the need for clear reporting to the ability of vulnerable states to plan and survive. The move connected technical process to existential stakes. The immediate outcome was modest. The longer-term effect was to anchor transparency debates in lived consequences rather than abstract compliance.

There are limits to this strategy, and island diplomats recognise them. Repeated invocation of vulnerability risks desensitisation. Larger states may harden positions or accuse small states of moralising. There is also the danger of being perceived as single-issue actors, marginalised when negotiations turn to implementation details. These risks are real.

Reconciling them requires discipline. Successful envoys modulate tone. They vary examples. They integrate vulnerability into broader arguments about efficiency, stability, and shared interest. They avoid absolutism. The ledger motif helps here. Accounts can be updated without dramatics. Precision sustains credibility.

Another limitation lies in the diversity of island experiences. Not all islands face identical risks. Some have higher elevations or more resources. Overgeneralisation weakens claims. Island coalitions address this by allowing variation within unity, presenting a range of cases that reinforce rather than dilute the central argument. The behaviour is differentiated solidarity. The explanation is credibility management. The consequence is resilience of the fairness frame.

Observable decisions reveal how leverage is exercised at the margins. Island states often insist on specific review mechanisms tied to sea-level metrics. They propose reporting on displacement and ecosystem loss alongside emissions. These proposals appear technical. They are strategic. Metrics institutionalise attention. Once measured, an issue resists erasure.

The ledger returns here. What is measured is owed attention. What is unmeasured fades.

As negotiations progress into finance and implementation, the leverage derived from risk reframing faces a test. Can moral authority translate into predictable support? Can loss be addressed without endless debate over liability? Island states navigate this by advancing proposals that balance principle with pragmatism: dedicated funding windows, insurance mechanisms, and multilateral facilities. The framing remains anchored in fairness, but the tools are operational.

The sharpened choice at the close confronts both island states and their counterparts. Treat climate risk as a distant probability to be managed gradually, or treat it as an ongoing loss that demands immediate accounting. The choice is not rhetorical. It shapes text, finance, and timelines. Island diplomats have learned how to force this choice onto the table, not by shouting, but by keeping the ledger open and insisting that each entry be read aloud.

Climate finance and loss debates

On 20 November 2022, in Sharm el-Sheikh, the final gavel of COP27 fell on an agreement to establish new funding arrangements for loss and damage. The hall exhaled. For small island states, the moment carried a precise weight. The commitment did not specify sums, formulas, or timelines. Yet after three decades of resistance, the principle had shifted. Climate harm was no longer treated solely as a risk to be mitigated or adapted to; it was recognised as damage requiring response. The United Nations Framework Convention on Climate Change had crossed a line. Money would follow, or credibility would drain away.

Finance is where climate diplomacy stops being symbolic.

The core argument of this section is clear. For small states, climate finance is not an accessory to ambition; it is the terrain on which ambition is judged. They insist on predictable, rules-based support because discretionary aid cannot underwrite survival in the face of recurrent loss. This insistence rests on a combination of legal reasoning, political realism, and lived arithmetic. It reframes climate finance from generosity to responsibility, without reciting equations.

Observation grounds the claim. Island states arrive at finance negotiations with a different temporal horizon. Adaptation projects span decades. Debt repayments fall annually. Storms arrive unpredictably. The behaviour is persistent: repeated calls for multi-year commitments, automatic triggers, and dedicated windows for the most vulnerable. The name for this posture is predictability preference. The explanation lies in fiscal fragility. The consequence is pressure on donors to move from pledges to systems.

Numbers sharpen the point. According to the World Bank's 2018 analysis, climate-related disasters impose average annual losses of 2–3 per cent of GDP on small island developing states, with single events often exceeding 20 per cent. For a large economy, such shocks are absorbed through borrowing or reallocation. For a microstate, they can erase years of investment overnight. When envoys speak of finance, they are speaking of continuity.

A five-word sentence captures it. Budgets cannot absorb surprises.

This reality drives a scepticism towards discretionary aid. Grants negotiated case by case, subject to shifting political priorities, do not align with recurrent loss. Island states have learned that unpredictability carries its own costs: delayed rebuilding, higher borrowing, and social strain. Their negotiating behaviour reflects this learning. They press for mechanisms that activate automatically when thresholds are crossed. The abstraction is insurance logic. The consequence is a reorientation of climate finance debates toward systems rather than projects.

Legal arguments support this shift. Small states draw on principles embedded in international environmental law:

common but differentiated responsibilities, the polluter pays principle, and the duty to prevent transboundary harm. They deploy these selectively, aware of sensitivities around liability. The behaviour is calibrated invocation. The explanation lies in strategic restraint. The consequence is legitimacy without provocation.

A case sketch illustrates how this plays out. In the lead-up to COP26 in Glasgow in 2021, a coalition of small island states worked through the Subsidiary Body for Implementation to propose a dedicated funding window within existing climate finance institutions for particularly vulnerable countries. The proposal avoided new legal obligations. It emphasised operational efficiency and moral coherence. Delegations shared talking points, divided outreach, and targeted sympathetic partners. The immediate outcome was deferment. The longer-term effect was agenda entrenchment. By COP27, the concept of a distinct channel for loss and damage had gained sufficient traction to underpin the Sharm el-Sheikh decision.

The ledger motif returns here. Finance debates resemble accounting disputes over who records which entry. Island states insist that loss be entered on the balance sheet, not left as a footnote. Once entered, it demands allocation. This insistence changes the conversation. It shifts attention from whether harm exists to how it is managed.

Adaptation finance sits alongside loss debates, with its own tensions. Adaptation is often framed as investment with returns. Sea walls protect assets. Early warning systems save lives. Island states support this framing but resist its limits. Not all harm is adaptable. Some losses are sunk. Reefs do not recover on project timelines. Cultural sites cannot be relocated. The observable behaviour is distinction-making. The explanation is experiential knowledge. The consequence is conceptual clarity that strengthens arguments for separate funding streams.

A second named example clarifies the politics. At COP24 in Katowice in 2018, Fiji, presiding over the conference, elevated the Talanoa Dialogue—a process grounded in storytelling and collective problem-solving. While not a finance mechanism, it altered the tone of discussions, allowing small states to link adaptation needs to broader narratives of responsibility. The dialogue did not resolve funding gaps. It did, however, soften resistance to later proposals by reframing finance as a shared endeavour rather than a transfer. Process influenced substance.

Critics raise a credible limitation. Predictable finance, they argue, risks creating dependency or inefficiency. Automatic triggers may disburse funds without adequate oversight. Dedicated windows may fragment institutions. These concerns are not dismissed lightly. Island states acknowledge them. Their response is pragmatic. Predictability does not preclude accountability. Systems can include review clauses, performance benchmarks, and sunset provisions. The trade-off is not between order and chaos, but between managed risk and unmanaged loss.

Observable adjustments reflect this reconciliation. Small states increasingly support blended mechanisms that combine grants with insurance payouts and concessional lending, tailored to shock type. They advocate for pre-agreed criteria rather than open-ended claims. The behaviour is design engagement. The explanation lies in credibility preservation. The consequence is broader acceptance of the underlying principle.

Debt weaves through these debates as a silent constraint. Climate shocks increase borrowing. Borrowing constrains adaptation. Small states have therefore linked climate finance to debt relief, arguing that funds recycled into repayments defeat their purpose. The political argument is direct: financing resilience while extracting debt service is self-defeating. The legal argument is subtler, invoking sustainable development obligations. Together, they press donors to consider net flows rather than gross pledges.

The ledger metaphor sharpens again. What matters is the bottom line.

Media narratives amplify these arguments when timed carefully. Island delegations often release analyses showing how pledged finance compares to disaster costs in specific years. The behaviour is comparative disclosure. The explanation is narrative discipline. The consequence is pressure on donors to justify gaps publicly.

Yet finance debates remain slow. Commitments lag. Trust frays. Island states operate in this environment with patience that is strategic, not passive. They understand that institutional change accrues incrementally. Text inserted here supports mechanisms there. A review clause today enables a facility tomorrow. Persistence is method.

The politics of responsibility require careful navigation. Explicit liability language triggers defensive reactions. Island envoys therefore focus on moral responsibility framed through cooperation rather than blame. They emphasise shared interest in stability, reduced migration pressures, and preserved ecosystems. The behaviour is reframing. The explanation lies in coalition maintenance. The consequence is widened support for funding solutions that might otherwise stall.

The section closes on a sharpened test for climate finance architecture. Will it continue to rely on episodic generosity, or will it evolve into a system capable of responding predictably to loss? For small states, the answer determines whether climate diplomacy translates into resilience or rhetoric. The ledger is open. Entries accumulate. At some point, settlement becomes unavoidable.

Profiles of climate envoys in action

On 21 September 2014, on the margins of the UN Climate Summit in New York, Tony de Brum of the Marshall Islands stood in a narrow corridor outside the General Assembly Hall and compared notes with delegates from countries thousands of times larger than his own. He was then seventy years old, a veteran of independence struggles and nuclear disarmament campaigns, and serving as Foreign Minister of a nation whose highest point barely cleared a few metres above sea level. The figure that followed him into the room was stark. According to the US National Oceanic and Atmospheric Administration's 2013 update, sea levels in parts of the western Pacific were rising at roughly three times the global average. De Brum carried that number lightly. He carried its consequences precisely.

People, not abstractions, move climate diplomacy in small states.

The argument of this section rests on a recurring empirical pattern. Climate envoys from microstates tend to share three characteristics: legal or quasi-legal training that equips them to work text and procedure; deep, continuing ties to the communities most affected by climate impacts; and unusually long tenures that allow expertise and relationships to compound. These traits do not arise by accident. They are adaptations to structural constraint. In systems where delegations are small and stakes existential, the individual becomes the institution.

Observation grounds the claim. In many island states, the same person who negotiates in Bonn or New York attends village meetings on return. The behaviour is cyclical: global forum, regional caucus, community hall, then back again. The name for this movement is translational diplomacy. The explanation lies in scale. When the distance between policymaker and affected citizen is short, translation is unavoidable. The consequence is a form of authority rooted in continuity rather than hierarchy.

Tony de Brum exemplified this pattern. Trained not as a lawyer but as a political organiser, he nonetheless mastered the language of treaties. His interventions at climate meetings rarely exceeded two minutes. They were spare. He often began with a local reference—waves breaking across the runway at Majuro, taro patches ruined by saltwater intrusion—before pivoting to the implications for international responsibility. The observable behaviour was disciplined brevity. The concept was moral clarity anchored in lived fact. The consequence was influence disproportionate to his state's size, visible in the formation of the High Ambition Coalition that helped secure stronger temperature goals in the Paris Agreement in 2015.

Legal training sharpens this craft. Many climate envoys from microstates come to diplomacy through law, environmental regulation, or public administration. This background fosters an instinct for text, precedent, and institutional process. Consider Ambassador Selwin Hart of Barbados, who served for years as his country's climate envoy before taking on a UN role in 2021. Hart's interventions often linked Caribbean hurricane data to draft decision language on adaptation and finance. The behaviour was evidentiary linkage. The explanation lay in legal habit: facts must attach to clauses. The consequence was a steady insertion of Caribbean realities into global frameworks that might otherwise have overlooked them.

Grassroots ties provide the second pillar. Climate diplomacy from microstates is sustained by continual reference back to place. Envoys attend funerals after storms. They walk eroded shorelines. They listen to fishers describe shifting currents. These experiences do not appear verbatim in negotiating text. They inform judgement. When an envoy insists that a proposed review period is too long, it is often because she knows how quickly another storm season will arrive. The abstraction is urgency. The metric is calendar time.

A brief vignette illustrates this translation at work. In October 2019, ahead of COP25 in Madrid, an ambassador from a low-lying Indian Ocean state returned from a coastal village where residents had marked the retreat of the shoreline by planting stakes each year. The line of stakes curved inland. At the conference weeks later, during a debate on loss and damage, she referred not to projections but to those markers, now partially submerged. She did not show photographs. She described the act of measuring. The room leaned in. The behaviour was narrative restraint. The explanation was trust in detail. The consequence was heightened attention to language recognising irreversible loss.

Long tenure completes the triad. In large diplomatic services, rotation is frequent. In microstates, continuity is a resource. An envoy who attends climate conferences for a decade acquires not only technical mastery but an intuitive sense of rhythm: when negotiations harden, when compromise becomes possible, when silence carries more weight than speech. The behaviour is timing. The explanation is accumulated experience. The consequence is leverage exercised without drama.

This accumulation also builds informal networks that matter. Climate negotiations run on official meetings and unofficial conversations. Envoys from small states who remain in post learn who drafts which paragraph, who influences which delegation, who listens late at night when formal channels stall. These insights do not appear in organisational charts. Biography captures them.

The motif that binds these profiles is the tide table. Island envoys read negotiations as sailors read tides. They know when to push and when to wait. They understand that force applied against the current wastes energy. The tide table is not guesswork; it is built from observation over time. Long tenure allows its compilation.

Another profile illustrates the point from a different angle. Ambassador Elizabeth Thompson of Barbados, a former minister with deep involvement in climate finance debates, combined political experience with legal fluency. During discussions on adaptation funding in the late 2010s, she frequently linked budget cycles in donor countries to hurricane seasons in the Caribbean. The behaviour was temporal alignment. The explanation lay in political realism. The consequence was proposals for financing mechanisms that matched need with disbursement timing.

These envoys also navigate a delicate representational burden. They are expected to speak for nations, regions, and sometimes for "the vulnerable" writ large. Overextension is a risk. Effective envoys manage this by anchoring claims narrowly, then allowing others to generalise. The behaviour is scoped advocacy. The explanation is credibility preservation. The consequence is sustained influence without dilution.

There are limits to biographical leverage. Individuals age. Burnout accumulates. Over-identification with a single figure can leave a vacuum when they depart. The death of Tony de Brum in August 2017 prompted concern among Pacific negotiators about continuity. The response was instructive. Younger diplomats stepped forward, mentored by those who had served alongside him. The craft was transferred. The tide table was shared. Biography here revealed both vulnerability and resilience.

Another limitation arises from domestic politics. Envoys operate within national mandates that can shift abruptly after elections. Long tenure does not guarantee insulation. When priorities change at home, even the most skilled negotiator must adjust. Biography explains adaptation under constraint, not immunity from it.

Reconciling these limits requires institutional support. Some microstates have begun to formalise knowledge transfer through small climate units or legal advisory panels, ensuring that individual expertise feeds collective memory. The behaviour is codification. The explanation lies in risk management. The consequence is reduced dependence on any single career.

Yet even with such structures, individuals remain unusually central. In a delegation of three, one person's illness can alter outcomes. This fragility sharpens performance. Envoys prepare meticulously because absence is felt immediately. The abstraction is responsibility. The metric is delegation size.

The tide table motif returns in how these envoys move between forums. A community meeting informs a regional position. A regional summit shapes a global intervention. A global decision reframes local expectations. The movement is continuous. Climate diplomacy here is not episodic; it is circulatory.

The persuasive power of local stories in plenary debates illustrates this circulation. When an envoy speaks of erosion, she often does so after testing the story with colleagues, ensuring it aligns with the point at issue. She avoids embellishment. She names dates. She connects the story to text. The behaviour is narrative calibration. The explanation is respect for the forum. The consequence is attention that translates into influence.

As climate negotiations become more technical, there is a risk that these human profiles fade behind acronyms and spreadsheets. This section argues the opposite. The more complex the machinery, the more decisive the craft of those who know how to work it. In microstates, that craft is embodied.

The sharpened choice at the close concerns succession. Will small states continue to rely on long-serving envoys who accumulate authority slowly, or will turnover erode hard-won leverage? The answer lies partly in institutions, partly in mentorship, and partly in recognising that in climate diplomacy, biography is not an anecdote. It is infrastructure.

Chapter 3
Maritime Law as Strategic Asset

At dawn on 7 August 2014, a small survey vessel idled just beyond the reef line of a Pacific island state whose land area barely exceeded that of a medium-sized city. The crew lowered sonar equipment into waters that had fed local communities for generations but had never been formally mapped to international standards. On shore, the foreign ministry waited for the data. Months later, that quiet exercise—funded through a modest technical grant and overseen by a handful of civil servants—would underpin a submission to the United Nations that secured jurisdiction over an expanse of ocean hundreds of times larger than the country's land territory. No flags were raised. No speeches made. Yet a boundary shifted, legally and durably.

For many island and coastal states, the sea is not scenery. It is territory by other means. Modern maritime law has transformed water into a domain of rights, obligations, and opportunities that often dwarf what lies above the high-water mark. For microstates, this transformation has been nothing short of structural. Where land is scarce, jurisdiction floats. Where borders on land are fixed, those at sea can be clarified, extended, defended, or, if neglected, quietly lost.

The paradox is striking. States with the smallest footprints on the map can possess some of the largest zones of legally recognised control. The mechanism is not force but law, patiently applied. This chapter explores how maritime law has become one of the most powerful strategic assets available to small nations, and why mastery of its technicalities has altered the balance between geography and power.

The law of the sea did not emerge fully formed. It is the product of decades of negotiation, codified most comprehensively in the United Nations Convention on the Law of the Sea, which entered into force in 1994. For large naval powers, the convention rationalised navigation and transit. For small coastal and island states, it opened an entirely new strategic horizon. Exclusive economic zones, continental shelf rights, and environmental jurisdictions transformed coastlines into launching points for sovereignty measured not in hectares but in nautical miles.

What matters here is not the text alone, but the work required to activate it. Rights on paper do not enforce themselves. They must be mapped, registered, defended, and, when challenged, argued. This labour is rarely dramatic. It involves hydrographic surveys, legal drafting, inter-ministerial coordination, and careful submissions to international bodies. It is also where small states often excel, precisely because the stakes are so concentrated.

Mapping is the first translation of geography into jurisdiction. A coastline drawn imprecisely can cost millions in fisheries revenue or mineral access over time. Small states have learned this lesson, sometimes the hard way. Investing in accurate surveys, often with external technical support, has become a priority not because it attracts attention, but because it prevents erosion of rights. A line drawn correctly once can shape decades of economic opportunity.

Registration follows. Submissions to bodies such as the Commission on the Limits of the Continental Shelf require meticulous preparation. Deadlines matter. Evidence must meet technical thresholds. For administrations with limited staff, this is demanding work. Yet it is also work that rewards focus. Unlike sprawling policy agendas, a maritime submission has a clear objective and measurable outcome. When successful, it delivers something few domestic policies can: internationally recognised control over resources.

Shipping adds another layer. Harbours, straits, and bunkering points sit at the junction of global commerce. Control over them does not require a navy; it requires regulation. Port state control allows governments to set conditions for entry, safety, and environmental compliance. Small states with well-placed ports have discovered that modest investments—in inspection capacity, waste facilities, or fuel standards—can influence which ships call, where they refuel, and how they operate.

These decisions ripple outward. A port that enforces strict environmental rules may deter older vessels while attracting newer fleets aligned with emerging standards. Traffic patterns adjust. Insurance calculations shift. What begins as a domestic regulatory choice acquires international consequences. The leverage lies not in exclusion, but in conditional access.

Maritime law also offers a forum for dispute resolution that favours preparation over intimidation. Specialised tribunals and arbitration panels provide avenues for clarifying boundaries and responsibilities without resorting to force. Small states often prefer these venues precisely because they substitute argument for armament. A well-prepared case can neutralise disparities in power by narrowing the question to interpretation rather than might.

There are instructive cases where microstates have pursued arbitration not to provoke conflict, but to stabilise relations. By clarifying a boundary or safety obligation, they reduce uncertainty for all parties. The immediate effect may be technical. The strategic effect is confidence. Investors, insurers, and neighbouring states adjust behaviour once rules are settled. Law, in this sense, creates predictability where power politics would produce tension.

The human dimension of this legal work matters. Behind successful maritime strategies stand lawyers and jurists who combine technical mastery with political awareness. They draft clauses with an eye to future disputes. They explain outcomes to domestic audiences who may see only abstract lines on charts. They cultivate networks with academics, surveyors, and colleagues abroad to keep pace with evolving interpretations. In small states, such individuals often carry extraordinary responsibility.

One such jurist, serving a coastal microstate, spent years studying obscure arbitration precedents related to canal transit and environmental protection. When negotiations arose over routing and safety standards for a proposed shipping shortcut, she drew on that research to argue that stricter controls were not only permissible but advisable under existing law. The argument reframed the discussion. What had seemed an economic concession became a legal obligation. The bargaining position shifted.

Throughout this chapter, the sea functions as a recurring motif. It appears as boundary, resource, highway, and courtroom. Its surface seems fluid, but beneath it lie fixed principles that reward those who understand them. Small states, often portrayed as at the mercy of larger currents, have learned to work with these principles, anchoring their interests in law rather than force.

Modern relevance sharpens the point. As maritime traffic intensifies, seabed resources attract attention, and environmental pressures mount, disputes over ocean space are likely to increase. Climate change complicates matters further, raising questions about baselines, erosion, and the persistence of maritime zones as coastlines retreat. For states whose future is inseparable from the sea, legal clarity becomes existential.

This chapter traces how small nations have turned maritime law into a strategic asset through quiet competence rather than confrontation. It moves from the technical work of defining zones, through the regulatory leverage of ports and shipping lanes, into courtrooms where precedents are forged, and finally into the careers of the lawyers who make these outcomes possible. The common thread is deliberate investment in rules that outlast any single negotiation.

The reader is invited to consider a simple but unsettling proposition. In a world where land is finite and power unevenly distributed, the most consequential expansions of sovereignty may occur not through conquest, but through survey lines, filings, and judgments. For small states, the ocean offers space. Law offers reach. Together, they redraw what influence can look like when size is no longer destiny.

Exclusive zones and sea borders

In April 2012, the government of Mauritius submitted a carefully prepared dossier to the United Nations Commission on the Limits of the Continental Shelf in New York. The land area of the country measures just over 2,000 square kilometres. The maritime claim it sought to secure extended across an area of ocean more than a thousand times larger. The figures were not rhetorical. They were the product of years of hydrographic surveys, sediment analysis, and legal drafting undertaken largely out of public view. When the Commission issued its recommendations later that year, Mauritius gained internationally recognised rights over vast seabed areas rich in fisheries and potential mineral resources. A small state had expanded its effective territory without moving a single border post.

This is the quiet arithmetic of the modern law of the sea. Land ends at the waterline. Jurisdiction does not.

The core proposition of this section is exact. Under contemporary maritime law, coastal and island states can lawfully convert surrounding waters into zones of enforceable rights that dwarf their terrestrial size. Exclusive economic zones and continental shelf claims do not arise automatically from geography; they are made real through technical work. Mapping, registration, and persistence translate coastlines into jurisdiction. For microstates, this translation has become one of the most consequential acts of statecraft available.

Observation makes the scale visible. An island with a landmass smaller than London can command authority over an exclusive economic zone extending 200 nautical miles from its shores. In practical terms, this can mean control over fisheries, seabed minerals, energy installations, and environmental regulation across millions of square kilometres. The name for this expansion is juridical reach. The explanation lies in treaty-based entitlement. The consequence is a redistribution of strategic weight that traditional maps conceal.

The United Nations Convention on the Law of the Sea, which entered into force in 1994, codified these entitlements. It established exclusive economic zones, recognised continental shelf rights beyond 200 nautical miles under certain conditions, and created mechanisms for boundary delimitation. For large states, the Convention rationalised existing practices. For small ones, it created opportunities that had never existed. Sea borders became as important as land borders, sometimes more so.

Yet entitlement alone does nothing. Rights unclaimed are rights eroded. Small states learned early that the law of the sea rewards those who act. Hydrographic data must be gathered. Baselines must be defined. Claims must be lodged before deadlines. Silence can be costly. A poorly defined boundary invites encroachment; an unregistered shelf invites competing narratives. The behaviour that distinguishes successful microstates is early, meticulous engagement.

A second example illustrates the point. In 2009, the Republic of Seychelles commissioned new marine surveys to clarify the extent of its continental shelf in the western Indian Ocean. The project was expensive relative to the national budget and politically unglamorous. The data collection took years. The payoff arrived quietly. In 2011, Seychelles and Mauritius made a joint submission that resulted in shared management of an extended continental shelf area rich in tuna stocks. The metric was square kilometres secured. The abstraction was cooperative sovereignty. The consequence was long-term control over resources central to national income.

Mapping is the first translation. Modern maritime claims rely on precise geospatial data. Coastlines are measured. Sediment thickness is analysed. Bathymetric profiles are plotted. For small administrations, this often requires external technical assistance. What matters is not ownership of technology, but command of process. States that understand what data is required, how it must be presented, and when it must be submitted gain disproportionate advantage.

Registration is the second translation. Submissions to international bodies convert data into recognition. The process is slow and procedural. It favours patience. Small states often excel here because the task, though complex, is finite. A dedicated team can focus on a single submission over several years. Large states, with broader agendas, sometimes struggle to sustain attention at this level of detail. The result is an inversion of expected advantage.

The motif binding these steps is the survey line. Drawn initially on charts, then embedded in legal text, the survey line becomes a durable expression of sovereignty. It does not attract attention. It endures. Once accepted, it shapes behaviour of fleets, investors, and neighbouring states. The survey line appears again and again in this chapter because it captures how quiet work produces lasting effect.

Exclusive economic zones also alter domestic governance. Control over waters creates obligations as well as rights. States must manage fisheries sustainably, police illegal activity, and regulate environmental impacts. For microstates, these tasks stretch capacity. Yet they also attract partnerships. Regional surveillance agreements, shared patrols, and cooperative management schemes emerge around clearly defined zones. Jurisdiction invites collaboration.

Sea borders introduce new diplomatic dynamics. Unlike land borders, they are rarely marked by fences or checkpoints. Enforcement depends on legitimacy and cooperation. A well-defined maritime boundary reduces friction by clarifying expectations. A vague one invites contest. Small states that invest in delimitation often do so to stabilise relations, not to provoke them. Clarity becomes a form of conflict prevention.

There is, however, a credible limitation. Not all states possess the administrative or financial capacity to pursue extensive maritime claims. Surveys cost money. Legal expertise is scarce. Competing domestic priorities intrude. Some microstates delay submissions and lose ground. Others submit incomplete data and face challenges. The law rewards preparation but punishes haste.

Reconciling this limitation reveals an important nuance. Capacity is not static. Small states have increasingly pooled resources, sharing survey vessels, legal advisers, and technical expertise. Regional organisations facilitate joint claims and coordinated timelines. The behaviour is collective investment. The explanation lies in economies of scale applied to law rather than production. The consequence is expanded access to maritime rights that would be unattainable individually.

Climate change complicates sea borders further. As coastlines erode and islands submerge, questions arise about the persistence of baselines. Can maritime zones endure if land disappears? Small island states have begun to press for legal interpretations that fix baselines permanently, decoupling maritime rights from shifting shorelines. This is not an abstract debate. It determines whether states retain jurisdiction over resources even as physical territory is threatened.

The observable behaviour here is anticipatory lawmaking. Envoys and legal advisers raise the issue in technical committees, scholarly forums, and draft resolutions. The explanation is existential foresight. The consequence may be a significant evolution in maritime law, driven not by major powers but by those most at risk.

Exclusive zones also intersect with economics in visible ways. Fisheries licensing provides revenue streams that can exceed domestic taxation in microstates. Control over seabed minerals attracts speculative interest. Renewable energy projects depend on clear jurisdiction. The metrics are licences issued, quotas enforced, contracts signed. These outcomes rest on lines drawn years earlier by surveyors few citizens ever meet.

The survey line returns here as both symbol and tool. It is drawn once, but it governs daily activity. It is defended not by force, but by reference. When disputes arise, states point to charts and filings. Arguments shift from power to proof.

The section closes on a sharpened choice that faces small coastal and island states. Invest early in defining and defending sea borders, or risk gradual erosion of rights through inattention. The choice is not dramatic. It is administrative. Yet its consequences are profound. In a world where land is finite and pressure on oceans intensifies, the most consequential expansions of sovereignty may continue to occur not through conquest, but through the careful drawing of survey lines that turn water into jurisdiction.

Shipping lanes and port access

On 29 March 2021, the *Ever Given* finally floated free in the Suez Canal after six days of paralysis. By then, according to Lloyd's List estimates published that week, nearly USD 60 billion worth of cargo had been delayed, insurance premiums had spiked, and hundreds of vessels were idling or diverting thousands of nautical miles around the Cape of Good Hope. Egypt did not need to threaten a single ship to feel the weight of its position. Geography had already done the work. Control of a narrow passage had translated instantly into global consequence.

Ports decide more than schedules.

The central argument of this section is precise. Control over harbours, straits, and bunkering points gives small states leverage over global shipping not through force, but through access. Port state control and access rights allow governments to set conditions under which vessels may enter, refuel, load, or wait. These conditions shape shipping behaviour at scale. Modest investments in facilities, inspection regimes, and regulatory standards can redirect traffic, alter cost structures, and influence norms far beyond national waters. For small states located at maritime crossroads, ports become instruments of diplomacy.

Observation clarifies how this works. Ships must stop. Crews must disembark. Fuel must be taken on. Waste must be discharged. Each of these necessities creates a point of contact between vessel and state. The behaviour is routine. The name for the authority exercised there is port state control. The explanation lies in jurisdiction. Once a ship enters a port, it accepts local rules. The consequence is leverage exercised quietly, ship by ship.

This leverage does not depend on fleet size or naval strength. It depends on positioning and reliability. A port that is safe, efficient, and predictable becomes valuable to shipping lines that operate on thin margins. A port that enforces standards consistently becomes influential. Small states understand this calculus acutely. When there is one main port, its performance becomes a national concern. When there are few alternatives nearby, access acquires weight.

A first example illustrates the dynamic. Singapore, though far wealthier than most microstates, demonstrates how port regulation translates into influence. By 2019, the Port of Singapore handled more than 37 million twenty-foot equivalent units, according to the Maritime and Port

Authority of Singapore. This scale was achieved not by lax regulation, but by meticulous standards for safety, bunkering, and environmental compliance. Ships calling at Singapore adapt to its rules because they must. The behaviour is compliance. The abstraction is norm diffusion. The consequence is regulatory influence radiating outward from a single harbour.

Smaller states replicate this logic on a different scale. Consider a coastal microstate with one deep-water port positioned along a busy regional route. By investing in modern inspection equipment and training inspectors to international standards, the government improves safety and reduces delays. Shipping lines respond by preferring the port over less reliable alternatives. Once traffic concentrates, the state gains room to adjust rules. The port becomes a gate.

The gate motif binds this section. Ports function as gates between sea and land. Gates can be opened wide, narrowed, or temporarily closed. The power lies not in slamming them shut, but in controlling their width. Shipping companies plan routes months in advance. Predictability matters. A gate that operates consistently commands attention.

Environmental standards have become a particularly potent way to adjust gate width. Port states can require vessels to meet emissions limits while berthed, to use cleaner fuels, or to comply with waste disposal rules. These measures appear technical. Their effects are strategic. Older, more polluting vessels are deterred. Newer fleets are encouraged. Over time, calling patterns shift.

A case sketch illustrates this effect. In 2018, the government of a Mediterranean island state revised environmental regulations for its main port, requiring ships to connect to shore power while at berth and imposing stricter controls on waste discharge. The port authority invested in basic infrastructure to support compliance. The immediate result was friction. Some operators complained. Within a year, however, cruise lines with newer vessels increased calls, while older ships diverted elsewhere. The metric was vessel age and emissions profile. The abstraction was selective access. The consequence was a cleaner port and enhanced bargaining position in negotiations with operators.

Port state control also interacts with international safety regimes. Inspections conducted under regional memoranda of understanding allow states to detain substandard vessels. For shipping companies, detention is costly. Reputational effects follow. A small state with a reputation for thorough, fair inspections can influence behaviour far beyond its waters. The behaviour is deterrence through enforcement. The explanation lies in networked compliance. The consequence is safer shipping and increased standing.

Straits magnify these effects. Narrow passages concentrate traffic. States bordering them may regulate transit for safety and environmental reasons. Even where freedom of navigation applies, cooperation with coastal authorities becomes essential. A state that manages vessel traffic services competently gains informational leverage. It sees flows before others do. It can signal risks, enforce standards, and shape expectations.

The second named example underscores this point. Turkey's administration of the Bosphorus Strait illustrates how safety regulation can shape strategic outcomes. By tightening traffic separation schemes and imposing scheduling controls, Turkish authorities have reduced accident risks in one of the world's busiest and most dangerous waterways. The behaviour is traffic management. The abstraction is chokepoint governance. The consequence is influence exercised through stewardship rather than coercion.

For small states, the lesson is transferable. While few control straits of such prominence, many sit astride regional routes or near refuelling points. Bunkering hubs, in particular, offer leverage. Fuel quality standards, pricing transparency, and safety rules affect where ships choose to refuel. States that set clear, credible standards attract compliant operators and exclude those unwilling to adapt.

Observable decisions reveal how this plays out. A government may choose to align port regulations with emerging international standards ahead of formal adoption. This early alignment signals direction. Shipping lines planning fleet upgrades take note. The port becomes future-proofed. The abstraction is anticipatory regulation. The metric is investment timing. The consequence is increased relevance over time.

There is, however, a credible limitation. Ports compete. Shipping lines can divert. A small state that tightens standards without offering reliability or efficiency risks losing traffic. Environmental ambition unaccompanied by operational competence backfires. This constraint disciplines policy choices.

Reconciling the limitation reveals a pattern. Successful small states sequence reforms. They invest first in reducing delays and improving services. They consult operators. They phase in standards predictably. The behaviour is calibrated enforcement. The explanation lies in commercial realism. The consequence is compliance without exodus.

Another limitation concerns capital. Port upgrades cost money. Microstates face tight budgets. The response has been selective investment. Rather than expanding capacity, governments focus on inspection quality, digital systems, and targeted infrastructure that unlocks leverage. The gate is refined, not enlarged.

The gate motif returns here. A well-designed gate does not need to be large. It needs to be reliable.

Port access also intersects with diplomacy directly. States use access as bargaining currency in bilateral talks. Preferential berthing rights, pilotage arrangements, or joint safety exercises create incentives for cooperation. These tools are quieter than tariffs or sanctions. They are often more effective.

Metrics make the effect tangible. Turnaround times measured in hours. Detentions counted per inspection. Fuel sulphur content recorded in parts per million. These numbers matter to operators. They also matter to diplomats, who translate them into arguments about responsibility and standards.

As global shipping confronts decarbonisation pressures, port leverage is likely to grow. New fuel requirements, shore power mandates, and emissions reporting will concentrate influence at ports capable of enforcing them. Small states that invest early position themselves as nodes in a changing network.

The section closes on a sharpened trade-off. Ports can be treated as passive infrastructure, or as active instruments of policy. For small states, the difference is strategic. By understanding ports as gates—points where global systems must pass through local rules—governments can exercise influence disproportionate to their size. The sea may be open. Access is not.

Maritime courts and arbitration cases

On 14 March 2012, in Hamburg, judges of the International Tribunal for the Law of the Sea took their seats to hear a case brought by Bangladesh against Myanmar concerning their maritime boundary in the Bay of Bengal. Bangladesh's land area is modest; its coastline short and vulnerable. The waters at stake extended across tens of thousands of square kilometres, rich in fisheries and energy potential. Bangladesh arrived with no fleet to project power, only a legal team carrying charts, sediment data, and years of preparation. Two days later, when the judgment was delivered, the Tribunal endorsed a boundary methodology that secured Bangladesh access to a significant maritime zone it had long feared losing. The courtroom was quiet. The effect was durable.

Courts change maps.

The central argument here is unambiguous. For small states, maritime courts and arbitration panels provide a strategic alternative to contests they cannot win by force. These forums privilege evidence, preparation, and interpretation over intimidation. When used with care, they allow microstates to clarify boundaries, establish safety obligations, and define environmental duties in ways that materially strengthen their negotiating position. Law becomes not a shield alone, but a lever.

Observation clarifies why these venues appeal. Naval posturing is expensive. Escalation is risky. Informal bargaining favours those who can absorb delay or impose cost. Legal proceedings invert these advantages. They compress disputes into defined questions, governed by agreed rules, before adjudicators trained to weigh argument rather than muscle. The behaviour is forum selection. The name for this strategy is juridification. The consequence is a rebalancing of asymmetry.

The law of the sea offers an unusually dense institutional landscape. The International Tribunal for the Law of the Sea, ad hoc arbitral tribunals constituted under Annex VII of the United Nations Convention on the Law of the Sea, and specialised arbitration panels provide multiple pathways to resolution. Small states often choose these routes because they are predictable. Timelines are set. Evidence requirements are known. Outcomes, while uncertain, are reasoned.

The Bangladesh–Myanmar case illustrates the pattern. Bangladesh faced a concave coastline that, under strict equidistance methods, threatened to compress its maritime entitlements. Its legal team advanced an argument grounded in equity and geological continuity, supported by expert testimony. The Tribunal accepted a modified approach. The observable behaviour was meticulous case-building. The explanation lay in doctrinal fluency. The consequence was access to resources that altered Bangladesh's long-term economic prospects and strengthened its voice in subsequent regional negotiations.

A second example reinforces the point from a different region. In July 2014, an arbitral tribunal constituted under UNCLOS issued its award in a case brought by the Philippines against China concerning the South China Sea. The Philippines is not a microstate, but it confronted a vastly larger power. The tribunal clarified the status of maritime features and affirmed environmental obligations. While enforcement remained contested, the ruling reshaped diplomatic discourse. Smaller Southeast Asian states cited it to support their own positions. The behaviour was norm creation. The abstraction was legal precedent. The consequence was a shift in negotiating baselines.

For microstates, the value of such cases often lies less in immediate compliance than in clarification. A judgment draws lines. It defines terms. It constrains what can be claimed plausibly thereafter. Even when an opposing party resists implementation, third parties—insurers, investors, neighbouring states—adjust their behaviour in response to clarified law. This secondary effect is where leverage accumulates.

Preparation is the decisive variable. Legal cases reward those who invest early in evidence. Hydrographic surveys, environmental impact data, and historical usage records become assets. Small states often build compact, specialised teams that work across ministries, supported by external counsel where necessary. The behaviour is integration. The explanation lies in capacity concentration. The consequence is coherence that larger bureaucracies sometimes lack.

The motif binding these dynamics is the chart. In maritime litigation, charts are not illustrations; they are arguments. Lines drawn with precision carry legal weight. Once endorsed by a tribunal, they enter the record. They circulate. They become reference points in later talks. The chart appears again and again because it captures how abstract law fixes itself to physical space.

Courts also clarify safety and environmental duties that extend beyond boundaries. Cases concerning vessel safety, pollution prevention, and resource management establish expectations for conduct in shared waters. Small states benefit from this clarity because it levels the field. Obligations apply regardless of fleet size. Enforcement remains uneven, but standards gain definition.

There is, however, a credible limitation. Litigation is slow and costly. It demands expertise that small administrations may struggle to sustain. Outcomes are not guaranteed. A poorly prepared case can entrench disadvantage. Moreover, courts decide narrowly. They cannot resolve every political dimension of a dispute.

Reconciling this limitation requires selectivity. Small states do not litigate everything. They choose cases where legal clarity offers strategic return, where facts are strong, and where the question presented is amenable to judicial reasoning. The behaviour is restraint. The explanation lies in risk assessment. The consequence is preservation of credibility.

Another limitation concerns enforcement. Courts lack police powers. Compliance depends on political will. Small states therefore use rulings as inputs to negotiation rather than endpoints. A favourable judgment strengthens their hand at the table. It does not replace diplomacy; it reshapes it.

A profile illustrates how this translation occurs. In a dispute involving a canal route vital to regional shipping, a coastal microstate relied on an obscure precedent concerning transit passage and environmental protection. Its lead jurist, trained in both domestic environmental law and international maritime law, identified a case decided years earlier that recognised states' authority to impose safety conditions in narrow waterways. By weaving that precedent into arbitration submissions, the legal team reframed the dispute. What had appeared as obstruction became compliance with established duty. The tribunal's reasoning echoed the argument. In subsequent negotiations, the state's position hardened from preference to obligation.

The observable behaviour here was doctrinal synthesis. The explanation lay in scholarly engagement. The consequence was leverage achieved without confrontation.

Maritime litigation also produces domestic effects. Governments must explain cases to their publics. This requires translation from legal language to lived stakes. Successful jurists perform a dual role: technician and advocate. They draft pleadings for judges and narratives for citizens. In small states, where public scrutiny is intense, this duality matters. Legitimacy at home supports persistence abroad.

Metrics make the effect tangible. Square kilometres confirmed. Safety zones established. Environmental obligations clarified. These outcomes feed into licensing decisions, patrol priorities, and diplomatic talking points. They endure beyond electoral cycles.

The chart motif returns here. Once drawn and defended, it anchors policy. It informs how ministries plan, how investors assess risk, how neighbours negotiate. The chart is quiet power.

As maritime disputes proliferate with increased competition for resources and sea space, courts and arbitration panels are likely to grow in importance. Climate change will introduce new questions about baselines and rights. Small states that have invested in legal capacity will be better positioned to shape answers.

The sharpened choice at the close concerns strategy. Confront power directly, or reframe the contest through law. For small states, the latter often offers a path to durable influence. The courtroom is not neutral ground. It favours those who prepare. When they do, maps change.

Lawyers who stretched ocean rules

On 2 April 2015, in Hamburg, the International Tribunal for the Law of the Sea delivered an advisory opinion requested by the Sub-Regional Fisheries Commission, an organisation representing seven West African coastal states. The question was technical: what obligations do flag states owe when their vessels engage in illegal, unreported, and unregulated fishing within another state's exclusive economic zone? The answer mattered enormously. For small coastal economies losing millions annually to distant-water fleets, enforcement at sea was uneven at best. The Tribunal's opinion clarified duties of due diligence that extended beyond territorial waters. Overnight, a legal argument became a practical tool. Nets were not hauled in Hamburg, but leverage was.

Lawyers redraw oceans.

The argument of this section is that maritime lawyers serving small states do far more than interpret existing rules. They extend, adapt, and sometimes stretch those rules to fit realities that the original drafters did not fully anticipate. Operating at the intersection of doctrine and diplomacy, they act as technicians who draft clauses with surgical precision and as advocates who translate outcomes for domestic audiences. Their influence rests on craft, networks, and an appetite for quiet persistence rather than spectacle.

Observation grounds this claim. In small states, the same lawyer may advise a minister in the morning, negotiate text in the afternoon, and brief parliament in the evening. The behaviour is multiplex. The name for this role is dual-hatted counsel. The explanation lies in capacity constraints. The consequence is an unusually direct line between legal interpretation and national policy.

These lawyers often begin as generalists. Over time, necessity pushes them towards specialisation. Maritime law rewards depth. It evolves through cases, advisory opinions, and scholarly debate. Keeping pace requires constant engagement. Lawyers from small states therefore cultivate networks that compensate for limited in-house resources. They attend academic conferences, maintain correspondence with scholars, and collaborate with colleagues abroad. Expertise becomes distributed rather than resident.

A first named example illustrates how such networks operate. The advisory opinion requested by the Sub-Regional Fisheries Commission drew on submissions from multiple member states, supported by external experts. Lawyers from countries such as Senegal and Sierra Leone coordinated positions, shared research, and aligned arguments. The observable behaviour was collective authorship. The abstraction was norm extension. The consequence was a clarified standard that member states could invoke in licensing negotiations and enforcement actions.

The technical work behind such outcomes is exacting. Lawyers must identify questions narrow enough to attract judicial engagement yet broad enough to matter. They must assemble evidence that meets evidentiary thresholds. They must anticipate counter-arguments. In small states, this work is often conducted by teams that could fit into a single office. The constraint sharpens focus.

The motif that binds these portraits is the footnote. In maritime law, footnotes matter. They contain precedents, reservations, and interpretive clues. Lawyers who stretch ocean rules read footnotes closely. They trace lines of reasoning across decades. They notice where language softened, where obligations were implied rather than stated. The footnote becomes a hinge.

A vignette illustrates how this attention pays off. During negotiations over transit rules for a proposed canal expansion in a narrow waterway, a jurist advising a coastal microstate identified an obscure passage in a 1990s arbitral award concerning environmental protection and transit passage. The case was rarely cited. Its holding was narrow. Yet the reasoning recognised that states bordering straits could impose certain safety conditions when justified by environmental risk. The jurist wove this precedent into draft language circulated among negotiating partners. What had been framed as an economic concession was reframed as compliance with established duty. The bargaining tone shifted. The canal proceeded under stricter conditions. The footnote had done its work.

The effectiveness of such moves depends on credibility. Lawyers from small states cannot afford frivolous claims. Overreach invites dismissal. Successful practitioners therefore calibrate ambition carefully. They stretch rules incrementally, anchoring arguments in text and precedent. The behaviour is measured innovation. The explanation lies in reputational economy. The consequence is trust that allows further extension.

A second named example underscores this pattern. In 2011, Mauritius and Seychelles concluded a treaty establishing a joint management area over an extended continental shelf.

Behind the political agreement lay extensive legal work translating UNCLOS provisions on shared shelves into operational arrangements. Lawyers drafted clauses governing licensing, revenue sharing, and dispute resolution. The agreement was unusual. It attracted attention from scholars and practitioners alike. The abstraction was cooperative sovereignty. The metric was shared jurisdiction over tens of thousands of square kilometres. The consequence was a model other small states could study.

These lawyers also perform an outward-facing role at home. Maritime law is abstract. Its benefits are delayed. Citizens may not immediately grasp why a boundary ruling or advisory opinion matters. Lawyers therefore act as educators. They explain how a line on a chart translates into fishing licences, jobs, and environmental protection. In small states, where publics are attentive and sceptical, this translation is essential to sustain political support for long legal campaigns.

Observable behaviour reveals this advocacy. Press briefings after judgments. Parliamentary testimonies outlining implications. Community meetings where lawyers answer questions about access and enforcement. The abstraction is legitimacy. The consequence is domestic buy-in that allows governments to persist in legal strategies whose payoffs are not immediate.

There are constraints. Maritime litigation and advisory processes are slow. Lawyers must manage expectations.

Not every case yields a clear win. Sometimes the value lies in clarification rather than expansion. Communicating this nuance at home is challenging. Overpromising undermines trust.

Reconciling this limitation requires candour. Effective jurists explain uncertainty without diminishing resolve. They emphasise process over outcome. The behaviour is expectation management. The explanation lies in political survival. The consequence is sustained institutional support.

Networks extend beyond academia. Lawyers from small states often build informal coalitions with peers from other jurisdictions. They exchange drafts, compare interpretations, and alert one another to emerging jurisprudence. Digital communication has intensified this practice. Expertise circulates faster. Isolation diminishes.

The footnote motif appears again here. Networks often form around shared readings of particular cases or articles. A new interpretation circulates. It is tested in conversation. It appears in a submission. If accepted, it enters the canon. Incremental change accumulates.

There is also a gendered dimension worth noting. Several prominent maritime lawyers serving small states are women who combine technical mastery with public engagement. Their visibility challenges assumptions about who speaks authoritatively on maritime affairs. In small administrations, where roles are less siloed, such figures often rise quickly. Their careers illustrate how constraint can accelerate opportunity.

A credible limitation remains. Reliance on a small cadre of legal experts creates vulnerability. If a key lawyer retires or leaves, capacity gaps emerge. Small states respond by mentoring juniors, embedding knowledge in archives, and institutionalising processes. The behaviour is succession planning. The explanation lies in fragility awareness. The consequence is resilience.

The stretching of ocean rules is not a revolt against law. It is fidelity to its purpose. Maritime law was designed to balance competing interests in a shared space. As pressures intensify—from resource extraction to climate change—interpretation must evolve. Small states, acutely exposed to these pressures, often stand at the forefront of this evolution.

Climate change introduces new questions that lawyers are already probing. How do baselines shift as coastlines erode? Can maritime zones persist if islands submerge? Lawyers from small island states have begun to argue for fixed baselines, citing stability and equity. These arguments draw on existing principles but push them further. The footnotes multiply.

The section closes on a sharpened choice that confronts small states and their advisers. Treat maritime law as static text to be applied defensively, or as a living framework to be shaped through careful argument. The lawyers profiled here choose the latter. With charts, footnotes, and patience, they extend the reach of small states across oceans, one precedent at a time.

Chapter 4
Debt, Aid and Financial Bargains

On a humid afternoon in September 2019, in a capital city where the finance ministry overlooked a harbour still scarred by the previous cyclone season, the minister sat with two files open on his desk. One contained the schedule of debt service payments due within the next six weeks. The other held an engineering assessment of a seawall that had begun to fail, its concrete fractured, its base undermined by storm surge. The numbers did not balance. Paying creditors would preserve access to markets. Repairing the wall would protect homes, a hospital, and the only coastal road linking the airport to the city. Both were defensible. Only one was affordable.

For many small states, debt is not an abstraction. It is a daily presence that shapes political choice.

The paradox at the heart of this chapter is simple and persistent. Small economies are urged to invest in resilience, infrastructure, and human capital, yet are constrained by debt burdens that absorb scarce fiscal space. Shocks arrive frequently—storms, commodity price swings, sudden drops in tourism—and each shock pushes borrowing higher. Over time, debt service becomes a permanent line item, crowding out the very investments that might reduce vulnerability. The result is a cycle that is economic in form, but deeply political in effect.

Debt overhang in microstates has distinctive features. Tax bases are narrow. Imports dominate consumption. Public sectors are often the main employers. A single disaster can erase a year's growth. The social weight of debt service is therefore felt more directly than in larger economies. When budgets tighten, cuts fall on clinics, schools, and maintenance. Citizens experience debt not through ratios, but through postponed repairs and stalled projects.

This chapter examines how small states navigate that constraint, not as passive recipients of aid or supplicants before creditors, but as negotiators who learn to bargain with limited leverage. It traces how finance ministries become diplomatic hubs, how narratives about reform and vulnerability are constructed, and how new links between climate risk and financial architecture are being forged. The story is not one of escape from debt, but of working within it to create room for choice.

The political economy of small-state debt resists simplification. Many microstates carry debt levels that would trigger alarm in larger countries, yet remain solvent because lenders assume eventual support from multilateral institutions or strategic partners. This assumption is double-edged. It sustains access to credit, but dulls urgency for structural solutions. Persistent debt becomes normalised. Elections revolve around distribution rather than sustainability. Ministers inherit obligations contracted long before their tenure.

The first theme explored here is the lived experience of debt overhang. Rather than reciting debt-to-GDP figures, the chapter focuses on how debt service shapes policy horizons. When a finance minister knows that a fixed share of revenue is pre-committed for years ahead, flexibility disappears. Promises shrink. Planning becomes defensive. Resilience investments, which pay off over decades, lose out to immediate obligations that cannot be deferred without consequence.

This constraint becomes acute after shocks. A hurricane damages infrastructure and erodes revenue simultaneously. Borrowing increases to rebuild. Debt service rises. Fiscal space narrows further. The cycle tightens. What looks like mismanagement from afar often reflects structural exposure. Understanding this context is essential to judging the bargaining positions small states bring to creditors.

Negotiating restructurings and relief is therefore not an episodic event, but a recurring skill. Small economies renegotiate with a complex mix of actors: commercial banks, bondholders, bilateral lenders, and multilateral institutions. Each group responds to different incentives. Legal tools such as maturity extensions or interest reductions matter less here than the narratives that accompany them. Creditors want assurance that relief will not be squandered. Governments need room to breathe.

This chapter explores how small states craft those narratives. Credibility emerges as a central asset. Finance teams emphasise reform plans, revenue measures, and governance improvements, even when implementation capacity is thin. Regional solidarity can amplify voice. When several states face similar pressures, coordinated positions carry weight. A restructuring framed as an isolated failure invites punishment; one framed as a systemic response to shared shocks attracts accommodation.

The linkage between climate risk and debt has begun to reshape these conversations. Small states increasingly argue that vulnerability, not just creditworthiness, should inform financial terms. The logic is straightforward. Climate shocks drive borrowing. Borrowing constrains adaptation. Breaking the loop requires integrating climate considerations into debt frameworks. This is not charity. It is risk reduction.

Proposals emerging from this logic are varied. Debt-for-nature swaps channel savings into ecosystem protection. Climate-resilient clauses allow payment deferrals after disasters. Concessional finance tied to adaptation investments reframes spending as prevention rather than indulgence. These ideas remain contested, but they signal a shift. Small states are no longer content to manage debt in isolation from the risks that generate it.

Aid occupies an ambiguous position in this landscape. Grants can provide relief without adding to debt, but they are often unpredictable and politically conditioned. Small states value aid that aligns with long-term priorities rather than donor cycles. They resist programmes that substitute for domestic capacity or fragment policy coherence. Aid, like debt, becomes a bargaining terrain where clarity and consistency matter.

At the centre of these negotiations stand finance ministers who operate as de facto foreign ministers. In small states, economic diplomacy is not delegated. The finance minister meets rating agencies, negotiates with development banks, briefs investors, and reassures domestic audiences. Personal credibility matters. A minister who communicates clearly, acknowledges constraints, and presents coherent plans can narrow the gap between borrower and lender.

This chapter follows such figures into meeting rooms far from home, where slide decks replace speeches and trust is built incrementally. A well-prepared presentation can reframe scepticism, shifting focus from headline debt levels to trajectories and reforms. The stakes are high. A downgrade can raise borrowing costs overnight. A positive signal can unlock financing on tolerable terms.

Throughout the chapter, a recurring image anchors the analysis: the balance sheet as shoreline. Each shock erodes it. Each restructuring rebuilds it, imperfectly. Finance ministers patrol this shoreline, aware that another storm is always forming offshore. Their task is not to eliminate exposure, but to reinforce defences where possible.

Modern relevance sharpens the theme. Global interest rates have risen. Climate impacts have intensified. Development finance is under strain. For small states, the margin for error has narrowed. The bargains they strike over debt, aid, and reform will shape not only economic outcomes, but political legitimacy and social cohesion.

The chapter that follows moves through these issues with an eye to practice rather than prescription. It traces choices made under pressure, compromises struck in asymmetrical settings, and innovations that emerged from necessity. It asks how small states convert limited bargaining power into workable financial space, and what that reveals about diplomacy when numbers matter as much as words.

The seawall from that minister's desk was eventually repaired, after payments were deferred and new terms negotiated. The relief was temporary. The lesson endured. In small states, finance is never just finance. It is diplomacy by other means, conducted under conditions where every decision leaves a visible mark on the shore.

Debt overhang in small economies

On 17 October 2018, in Roseau, Dominica, the finance minister signed off a payment to external creditors while the capital still bore the marks of Hurricane Maria, which had struck the island the previous year. The storm caused damage estimated at more than 200 per cent of annual GDP, according to the Government of Dominica's Post-Disaster Needs Assessment published with the World Bank in 2017. Roofs remained patched with tarpaulin. Schools operated on shortened hours. The seawall along Bayfront Road had cracked again under successive storm surges. The payment was due regardless. Debt does not pause for debris.

Debt overhang in small economies is not primarily a financial condition. It is a political climate.

The thesis of this section is direct. In microstates and very small economies, persistent debt service exerts a gravitational pull on public life that reshapes policy, constrains imagination, and hardens trade-offs between immediate survival and long-term resilience. Narrow tax bases, import dependence, and repeated shocks combine to make indebtedness chronic rather than cyclical. The burden is carried not in balance sheets alone, but in deferred repairs, stalled reforms, and quiet exhaustion within public institutions.

Observation grounds this claim. Small economies raise revenue from limited sources: consumption taxes, import duties, a handful of sectors such as tourism or fisheries. Volatility is built in. When a shock hits, revenues fall just as spending needs rise. Borrowing fills the gap. The behaviour repeats. The name for this condition is structural exposure. The explanation lies in scale and openness. The consequence is debt that persists even when governments act prudently.

Import dependence intensifies the pattern. Food, fuel, and construction materials are purchased abroad, often in foreign currency. Price spikes transmit instantly into domestic budgets. Subsidies rise. Foreign exchange drains.

Fiscal buffers thin. In such contexts, debt is not accumulated to fund extravagance, but to maintain continuity. The political narrative of profligacy misreads the arithmetic of necessity.

The social weight of debt service becomes visible in budget calendars. Payments to creditors are scheduled months in advance. They arrive with certainty. Expenditure on maintenance, training, or preventative care remains flexible, and therefore vulnerable. Over time, this asymmetry shapes public services. Roads are patched rather than rebuilt. Clinics operate with ageing equipment. Teachers wait for training that never arrives. Debt crowds out resilience quietly.

A five-word sentence captures it. Interest arrives before storms.

The example of Dominica is instructive, but not unique. After Cyclone Pam struck Vanuatu in March 2015, causing damage estimated at around 64 per cent of GDP by the Asian Development Bank that year, the government faced similar choices. Rebuilding required borrowing. Debt service rose. Climate vulnerability increased. The sequence repeated. Observed from afar, debt levels appeared unsustainable. Observed from within, they appeared unavoidable.

The political implications are profound. Persistent debt narrows policy horizons. Ministers learn to think in twelve-month increments. Long-term investments that would reduce vulnerability struggle to compete with immediate obligations. Electoral politics adapt. Promises become modest. Ambition is rationed. The public senses constraint, even when leaders avoid technical language.

Debt overhang also affects state capacity. Skilled civil servants spend increasing time managing cash flow, negotiating payment schedules, and reporting to lenders. Less time remains for planning or innovation. Burnout becomes common. Institutional memory thins as staff rotate or leave. The abstraction is capacity erosion. The consequence is diminished ability to escape the cycle.

A second example sharpens the point. In 2020, Barbados completed a high-profile debt restructuring after years of fiscal strain. The country's economy is larger and more diversified than many microstates, yet the social experience was familiar. Austerity measures affected public employment and services. Trust was tested. The restructuring created space, but only after sustained political effort. Smaller states face similar pressures with fewer buffers.

The seawall dilemma illustrates how debt shapes concrete choices. A damaged seawall is not merely infrastructure; it protects hospitals, roads, and livelihoods. Repairing it reduces future losses. Yet the benefits accrue over time, while the cost is immediate. Debt service, by contrast, offers no visible return to citizens, only the avoidance of penalty. Finance ministers weigh these options under scrutiny from lenders and voters alike. The choice is stark and recurrent.

This dynamic explains why resilience investments are chronically underfunded in small economies. It is not ignorance. It is arithmetic under constraint. Debt service claims first call on revenue. Resilience competes for what remains. When shocks recur, the logic reinforces itself. Borrow to rebuild. Pay to maintain access. Delay prevention.

There is a credible limitation to this account. Some small states have managed debt prudently and built buffers. Fiscal discipline matters. Governance quality varies. Debt overhang is not destiny. Acknowledging this matters to avoid fatalism.

Reconciling the limitation requires nuance. Discipline can mitigate, but not erase, structural exposure. Well-managed small states still face shocks beyond their control. The difference lies in degree, not kind. Those with stronger institutions negotiate better terms, rebuild faster, and retain credibility. They do not escape vulnerability; they manage it more effectively.

Observable behaviours distinguish these cases. Governments that publish transparent budgets, maintain consistent policy signals, and engage early with creditors fare better. The abstraction is trust. The metric is borrowing cost. The consequence is marginally wider room for manoeuvre.

Debt overhang also shapes foreign policy. Small states become sensitive to the preferences of major creditors and donors. Diplomatic positions may soften. Voting patterns may shift. This is not corruption. It is constraint translated into caution. Economic dependence bleeds into political calculation.

The motif binding this section is the tide gauge. Debt levels rise and fall like water against a seawall. After a storm, the gauge spikes. Over time, it recedes, but rarely returns to its previous mark. Each cycle leaves residue. The gauge becomes the background against which all decisions are measured.

Climate change intensifies this pattern. Storms become stronger. Recovery periods shorten. Debt accumulates faster than repayment. The tide gauge climbs. Finance ministers read it daily, aware that another surge is likely. Their task is not to stop the tide, but to prevent overtopping.

The section closes on a sharpened choice faced by small economies. Continue treating debt as a series of isolated problems to be managed year by year, or confront it as a structural condition requiring political, diplomatic, and financial innovation. The choice is difficult. It demands honesty with citizens and firmness with creditors. It also demands recognition that resilience postponed is vulnerability compounded.

The seawall in Roseau was eventually repaired, using a mix of concessional finance and deferred payments. It held during the next storm season. Debt service resumed. The gauge fell slightly. The cycle continued. Understanding that cycle, and its weight on small economies, is essential to grasping how they bargain, plan, and survive in a world where shocks arrive faster than relief.

Negotiating restructurings and relief

On 7 June 2018, in Bridgetown, Barbados announced it would suspend payments on most of its external debt. The declaration was stark, the timing deliberate. Public debt had climbed to levels that crowded out basic services, and foreign exchange reserves were thinning. Within weeks, representatives of banks, bondholders, and official lenders were in talks with a finance team whose mandate was as political as it was technical. By October 2019, Barbados had completed one of the most comprehensive restructurings in its history, extending maturities, lowering interest costs, and creating fiscal space measured not in theory but in reopened clinics and repaired roads. The island did not escape debt. It re-shaped it.

Restructuring is not an admission of failure. It is a negotiation about time.

The thesis of this section is straightforward. For small economies, debt restructurings are less about mathematical optimisation than about narrative credibility and strategic sequencing. Tools such as maturity extensions, interest reductions, or payment deferrals matter, but they succeed only when embedded in a convincing account of future reform and growth. Because leverage is thin and reputations are fragile, small states must negotiate not only with creditors' balance sheets but with their expectations.

Observation grounds this claim. When a microstate approaches creditors, the asymmetry is obvious. Lenders are diversified; borrowers are not. Delay hurts the debtor faster. This reality shapes behaviour. Small economies tend to act early, signalling distress before reserves are exhausted. The name for this posture is pre-emptive engagement. The explanation lies in risk containment. The consequence is a greater chance of cooperation rather than confrontation.

The mechanics of restructuring are often misunderstood. Extending maturities spreads payments over a longer horizon. Lowering interest rates reduces annual pressure. Grace periods create breathing space. These tools are familiar. What distinguishes small states is how sparingly they can deploy them. There is little room for miscalculation. A single missed payment can close markets for years.

Credible narrative therefore becomes the core currency. Finance teams construct stories about where the economy has been, why it reached its current position, and how it will change. These stories must be coherent, modest, and internally consistent. Overpromising destroys trust. Under-explaining invites suspicion. The behaviour is calibrated storytelling. The explanation lies in reputational economics. The consequence is the difference between relief granted and relief denied.

Barbados again offers an instructive case. The restructuring was accompanied by a clear reform programme focused on fiscal discipline, state-owned enterprise reform, and growth through renewable energy and tourism diversification. The government communicated regularly with creditors and the public. Transparency was not an afterthought; it was a tactic. The result was unusually high participation rates among bondholders, according to the International Monetary Fund's 2019 assessment, and a restructuring that restored stability without prolonged litigation.

Small economies also negotiate with official lenders, where politics enters overtly. Multilateral institutions balance financial prudence with developmental mandates. Bilateral lenders weigh strategic relationships. Small states must align their requests with these logics. The behaviour is forum differentiation. The explanation lies in institutional pluralism. The consequence is tailored appeals that avoid one-size-fits-all demands.

Regional solidarity can amplify these efforts. When several small economies face similar shocks, collective positioning strengthens arguments for exceptional treatment. After the global financial crisis of 2008 and again during the COVID-19 pandemic, small island states coordinated calls for debt relief and payment moratoria. The G20's Debt Service Suspension Initiative in 2020 reflected this pressure, even if its reach was limited. The abstraction was collective vulnerability. The metric was temporary fiscal space. The consequence was short-term relief that, while incomplete, demonstrated the value of acting together.

A case sketch illustrates this dynamic. In the eastern Caribbean, a group of states affected by successive hurricanes in the late 2010s coordinated engagement with regional development banks and bilateral creditors. By presenting shared data on disaster impacts and recovery costs, they reframed their requests from individual failures to systemic exposure. The resulting packages varied by country, but terms were more generous than those initially offered. Solidarity did not erase differences. It altered tone.

Negotiations also hinge on timing. Approaching creditors immediately after a shock can attract sympathy but risks appearing opportunistic. Waiting too long signals denial. Successful teams read the moment carefully. They engage informally first, testing reactions, adjusting proposals, and only then formalising talks. The behaviour is sequencing. The explanation lies in social dynamics of bargaining. The consequence is reduced resistance.

There is a credible limitation to this approach. Not all creditors respond to narrative. Some are constrained by mandates or domestic politics. Litigation remains a risk. For small states with bonds governed by foreign law, holdout creditors can extract concessions. The asymmetry resurfaces.

Reconciling this limitation requires institutional design. Collective action clauses in bond contracts, increasingly standard after 2014, reduce holdout risk. Engagement with the IMF or similar institutions can anchor negotiations, providing a framework that reassures creditors while constraining demands. The behaviour is architecture-building. The explanation lies in rule-setting. The consequence is fewer veto points.

Restructuring is also a domestic political act. Governments must justify concessions to citizens who may see negotiations as capitulation. Leaders therefore frame relief as reclamation of agency rather than surrender. Language matters. Payments are deferred to rebuild. Interest savings are invested in services. The abstraction is sovereignty regained. The consequence is public tolerance for difficult adjustments.

Observable behaviours reinforce this framing. Governments publish restructuring terms. They link savings to visible projects. They explain trade-offs candidly. In small societies, opacity is costly. Trust erodes quickly. Successful negotiators treat domestic communication as part of the deal, not a footnote.

The motif binding this section is the bridge. Restructuring builds a bridge between an unsustainable past and a plausible future. The bridge must be sturdy enough to carry reform, yet light enough to be acceptable to creditors. Too ambitious, and it collapses. Too timid, and it leads nowhere. Negotiators walk this bridge under scrutiny.

Climate risk increasingly features in these narratives. Small states argue that future growth depends on resilience investments that require fiscal space now. Creditors, aware of rising disaster risks, are more receptive to this logic than a decade ago. Debt instruments linked to climate outcomes have begun to appear, though unevenly. The behaviour is narrative evolution. The explanation lies in shared risk recognition. The consequence is incremental innovation.

Metrics anchor these claims. Disaster frequency. Insurance premiums. Repair costs. When presented clearly, they shift discussions from morality to prudence. Creditors are not asked to forgive out of generosity, but to invest in stability.

The section closes on a sharpened trade-off. Restructuring can restore room to manoeuvre, but it carries reputational cost. Avoiding it preserves appearance but drains capacity. Small states must choose when to absorb stigma in exchange for sustainability. Those that negotiate early, tell credible stories, and act collectively increase their chances of crossing the bridge without collapse.

Debt relief does not end dependence. It reorders it. For small economies, the art lies in using that reordering to buy time—time to reform, to invest, and to prepare for the next shock that, inevitably, waits offshore.

Linking climate, debt and reform

On 14 October 2021, in Bridgetown, Barbados launched what its prime minister called the Bridgetown Initiative, a proposal aimed at reshaping how international finance responds to climate vulnerability. The document was technical in places and political throughout. Its most arresting datum was simple: countries facing the highest climate risks often paid more to borrow than countries contributing most to the damage. Credit scores rewarded income and punished exposure. Storms did not register. The initiative argued that this mismatch was no longer tenable. Debt, climate, and reform had to be treated as one system.

Vulnerability does not appear on balance sheets.

The central claim of this section is that for small states, separating climate adaptation from debt management is a category error. Climate shocks drive borrowing. Borrowing constrains adaptation. Reform efforts that ignore this loop fail to break it. Linking climate, debt, and reform is therefore not a policy preference but a necessity born of arithmetic. Small states have begun to articulate this linkage with increasing clarity, pressing for financial frameworks that recognise vulnerability alongside creditworthiness.

Observation grounds the argument. When a hurricane destroys roads and power lines, governments borrow to rebuild. Debt service rises. Fiscal space shrinks. Investment in stronger infrastructure is delayed. The next storm inflicts greater damage. The behaviour is cyclical. The name for this condition is shock compounding. The explanation lies in exposure without buffers. The consequence is a ratchet effect that pulls states deeper into debt precisely because they are trying to recover.

Traditional financial metrics struggle with this reality. Credit ratings assess past performance and fiscal indicators. They rarely account for future climate risk in a systematic way. For small island states, this creates a perverse outcome. Countries that invest heavily in resilience may see debt rise in the short term and ratings fall, increasing borrowing costs. The abstraction is mispriced risk. The consequence is disincentive to invest in prevention.

Small states have responded by reframing the debate. Rather than pleading exceptionalism, they argue efficiency. Money spent on resilience reduces future losses. Lower losses reduce borrowing needs. Lower borrowing improves credit profiles. The logic is cumulative. The challenge lies in translating it into instruments that lenders accept.

One such instrument is the debt-for-nature swap. These arrangements allow a portion of a country's debt to be reduced or restructured in exchange for commitments to protect ecosystems. The most cited example remains the 2016 Seychelles debt swap, facilitated by The Nature Conservancy. Under the arrangement, part of Seychelles' external debt was restructured, and the savings were directed into marine conservation and the establishment of marine protected areas. The metric was debt reduced. The abstraction was ecological investment. The consequence was long-term protection of fisheries central to the economy.

What matters here is not novelty but design. The Seychelles swap worked because it aligned incentives. Creditors reduced exposure. Conservation groups achieved protection. The government gained fiscal space. The ecosystem provided resilience. Each party could justify participation to its constituency. This alignment has become a reference point for other small states exploring similar arrangements.

Another example illustrates the evolution of the idea. In 2020, Belize completed a debt restructuring that included a conservation component linked to its barrier reef. While the context differed, the principle was consistent: freeing fiscal space to invest in assets that underpin economic stability. The behaviour was instrument adaptation. The explanation lay in precedent learning. The consequence was wider acceptance of climate-linked debt solutions.

These instruments remain limited in scale. They do not solve systemic debt problems. Small states recognise this. Their push has therefore broadened from project-level swaps to framework-level reform. Proposals include climate-resilient debt clauses that allow automatic payment suspension after disasters, and concessional financing tied explicitly to adaptation outcomes. The aim is not forgiveness, but predictability.

Observable behaviours reveal how this advocacy unfolds. Finance ministers and climate envoys present integrated arguments in meetings with multilateral banks, linking disaster data to debt trajectories. They circulate joint papers through regional groupings. They engage rating agencies directly, challenging assumptions and sharing methodologies. The abstraction is narrative integration. The consequence is gradual shift in discourse.

A credible limitation must be acknowledged. Integrating climate risk into debt frameworks introduces complexity. Lenders worry about moral hazard. How are shocks defined? Who verifies impacts? How often can clauses be triggered? These concerns are not trivial. Poorly designed instruments could undermine market confidence.

Reconciling this limitation requires precision. Small states have responded by proposing objective triggers based on independent data sources, such as internationally recognised disaster declarations or parametric insurance thresholds. They accept caps and review periods. The behaviour is risk-sharing design. The explanation lies in credibility preservation. The consequence is instruments that attract cautious interest rather than outright rejection.

Reform also demands domestic alignment. Fiscal space freed by debt relief must be used visibly and effectively. Otherwise, trust evaporates. Governments therefore tie relief to specific investments: seawalls, early warning systems, social protection programmes. They report progress. Transparency becomes part of the bargain.

The motif binding this section is the circuit. Climate shocks, debt, and reform form a closed loop. Breaking it requires inserting resilience into the circuit, not treating it as an external add-on. Each intervention must reinforce the others. The circuit image appears again because it captures the system-level nature of the challenge.

This reframing has begun to influence multilateral discourse. Institutions such as the International Monetary Fund and World Bank have increased attention to climate vulnerability in their assessments, though unevenly. Pilot programmes emerge. Language shifts. The pace frustrates small states. Yet the direction matters. Norms change slowly, then suddenly.

Another dimension concerns social protection. Climate shocks disproportionately affect the poor. Linking debt relief to social spending protects political stability and human capital. Small states emphasise this connection, arguing that resilience is not only physical but social. The behaviour is broadened framing. The explanation lies in lived experience. The consequence is more holistic reform proposals.

Metrics again anchor the argument. Reduced disaster losses. Faster recovery times. Stable debt trajectories. When tracked consistently, these indicators make the case that resilience investments pay for themselves. They shift debate from compassion to prudence.

The section closes on a sharpened choice facing the international financial system. Continue to treat climate risk as an external shock to be managed episodically, or integrate it into the core logic of debt and reform. For small states, the choice is existential. Their advocacy reflects not impatience, but clarity about cause and effect.

Linking climate, debt, and reform does not eliminate vulnerability. It rearranges it. It shifts resources from reaction to preparation, from crisis to capacity. For small states standing at the edge of rising seas and tightening budgets, that shift marks the difference between permanent emergency and managed risk.

Finance ministers as chief diplomats

On 22 February 2022, in Washington, DC, a finance minister from a Caribbean microstate faced a room of sceptical analysts at a major multilateral bank. The agenda allowed fifteen minutes. The minister opened a slide deck with a single chart: hurricane landfalls over twenty years plotted against fiscal balances. The room quietened. The second slide showed debt service dates aligned with storm seasons. No rhetoric followed. By the end, the questions had shifted from *why are you asking* to *how can this be structured*. The meeting did not resolve everything. It changed the temperature. The currency was clarity.

Finance ministries are embassies now.

The thesis of this section is precise. In small states, finance ministers function as chief diplomats on economic matters because the decisive conversations about sovereignty, risk, and room to manoeuvre occur in financial forums. Relationships with multilateral banks, rating agencies, and major investors shape policy space more directly than many traditional alliances. Personal credibility and disciplined communication narrow the distance between small borrowers and large lenders, translating vulnerability into negotiated tolerance.

Observation grounds the claim. A microstate's foreign ministry may have a handful of officers. Its finance ministry, by contrast, maintains constant contact with actors whose decisions move markets overnight. The behaviour is continuous engagement. The name for this role is economic diplomacy. The explanation lies in exposure: financing terms determine whether governments can act. The consequence is a shift in where diplomacy happens and who conducts it.

The work is relational before it is technical. Multilateral banks and rating agencies prize consistency. Investors prize predictability. Finance ministers from small states therefore cultivate trust over time, often with the same interlocutors across years. They remember names. They answer emails promptly. They disclose problems early. The abstraction is credibility. The metric is access. The consequence is patience granted when shocks hit.

Consider the relationship with rating agencies. For small states, a downgrade can raise borrowing costs sharply, even when underlying conditions are stable. Finance ministers engage agencies not to lobby for leniency, but to ensure understanding. They explain fiscal calendars, disaster exposure, and reform sequencing. They correct misinterpretations. The behaviour is narrative maintenance.

The explanation lies in information asymmetry. The consequence is fewer surprises.

A named example clarifies the point. After Barbados embarked on its reform programme in 2018, then finance minister Ryan Straughn held regular briefings with rating agencies, outlining progress and setbacks candidly. According to agency reports published in 2019, this transparency informed assessments of policy credibility. Ratings did not improve immediately. They stabilised. For a small economy, that stability mattered.

Multilateral banks present a different diplomatic theatre. Here, ministers navigate governance structures where votes are weighted and mandates are broad. Influence accrues to those who speak the language of the institution while advancing national interest. Finance ministers prepare meticulously. They align proposals with institutional priorities—resilience, inclusion, sustainability—without diluting substance. The behaviour is alignment. The explanation lies in agenda setting. The consequence is proposals heard rather than shelved.

The slide deck vignette captures this craft. Data replaces exhortation. Charts are chosen for legibility, not volume. Ministers anticipate objections and address them pre-emptively. They frame requests as solutions to shared problems. When done well, scepticism softens into problem-solving. The meeting becomes a negotiation rather than an audition.

Investors demand another register altogether. Here, time horizons shorten and language sharpens. Finance ministers present roadmaps rather than visions. They specify triggers, milestones, and contingencies. They avoid promising outcomes they cannot control. The behaviour is disciplined forecasting. The explanation lies in reputational risk. The consequence is capital that remains engaged rather than fleeing at the first sign of stress.

The dual role requires translation. What reassures a development bank may alarm a hedge fund. What satisfies a domestic audience may unsettle creditors. Finance ministers toggle registers constantly, adjusting emphasis without changing facts. This translation is labour-intensive. In small states, it often falls on the minister personally. There is little buffer.

The motif binding this section is the bridge. Finance ministers build bridges between disparate worlds: domestic politics and global finance, disaster reality and spreadsheet logic. A bridge must carry weight in both directions. If it sways, traffic slows. If it holds, movement continues.

A second named example illustrates bridge-building under pressure. In the aftermath of Cyclone Pam in 2015, Vanuatu's finance leadership engaged donors and lenders to secure emergency financing while maintaining debt sustainability. According to Asian Development Bank reports that year, the government communicated clearly about priorities and constraints, enabling rapid disbursement of concessional funds. The abstraction was trust under stress. The metric was time to cash. The consequence was recovery without destabilising debt.

Personal credibility amplifies institutional messages. Ministers who acknowledge uncertainty, admit missteps, and correct course publicly accrue trust. Those who obscure or deflect lose it quickly. In small states, reputations travel fast. A single meeting can shape years of engagement.

This reliance on individuals introduces risk. Turnover can disrupt relationships. Elections can reset narratives. There is a credible limitation here. Economic diplomacy concentrated in one office can become brittle.

Reconciling the limitation requires institutionalisation. Successful small states document engagements, train deputies, and maintain continuity across political cycles. They build teams that can sustain relationships when ministers change. The behaviour is redundancy building. The explanation lies in resilience. The consequence is reduced dependence on any one personality.

Yet individuals still matter. When crises hit, counterparts want a human voice. They want someone accountable. Finance ministers step into that space. Their presence signals seriousness. Their absence is noticed.

The bridge motif appears again in crisis management. During the COVID-19 pandemic, finance ministers from small states spent countless hours on calls with lenders, explaining revenue collapses and requesting flexibility. Those with established credibility secured deferrals faster.

According to IMF programme documents from 2020, early engagement correlated with smoother adjustments. The pattern repeated across regions.

Clarity is the common denominator. The best economic diplomats do not overwhelm. They select evidence. They connect cause and effect. They respect the listener's constraints. Clarity does not guarantee agreement. It creates the conditions for it.

There is also a domestic diplomatic dimension. Finance ministers must carry their publics with them. Restructurings, conditionalities, and reforms impose costs. Explaining why a meeting in a distant capital matters to daily life is part of the job. Ministers who communicate well domestically strengthen their hand abroad. Creditors watch domestic politics closely.

Observable behaviours illustrate this feedback loop. Town hall briefings after international meetings. Parliamentary statements linking outcomes to services. Transparency reports tracking commitments. The abstraction is legitimacy. The consequence is political space to negotiate.

As climate risk intensifies, the role of finance ministers as diplomats will deepen. Negotiations over climate finance, insurance, and debt instruments require fluency across domains. Ministers must speak climate and capital with equal ease. Small states that invest in this fluency gain leverage disproportionate to size.

The section closes on a sharpened choice. Treat finance as a technical silo, or recognise it as a primary arena of diplomacy. For small states, the choice has already been made by circumstance. Finance ministers are envoys by necessity. Their tools are charts, narratives, and trust. When wielded with care, these tools do not eliminate constraint. They convert it into negotiable space, one meeting at a time.

Chapter 5
Tourism, Brands and Soft Power

On a quiet morning in February 2016, a foreign ministry official in a Pacific island capital opened an email from a major international news outlet. The subject line referred to a polluted beach—photographs already circulating online, comments accumulating beneath them. Tourism arrivals had dipped before. This felt different. Within hours, the government contacted the resort operator responsible for the stretch of coastline. The message was calm, precise, unmistakable. Remediation would begin immediately, or the state would go public. By the following week, heavy equipment was on the sand, contractors working at dawn. The story did not disappear. It changed direction.

For small states, visibility is never neutral.

Tourism-dependent economies live in a paradox. Their prosperity relies on openness: flights arriving on time, cruise ships docking, images of sunlit water circulating freely. That same openness exposes them to volatility they do not control. Airlines reroute. Travel advisories shift. A single viral image can undo months of marketing. Dependence on visitors brings revenue and employment, but it also imports fragility. Yet to treat tourism only as a vulnerability is to miss its political potential.

This chapter explores how small states convert exposure into influence. It examines tourism not merely as an industry, but as a platform for soft power: a means of shaping perceptions, setting agendas, and negotiating outcomes beyond the beach. Where previous chapters traced leverage through law, finance, and institutions, this one follows it through brands, culture, and carefully managed attention.

The scale of reliance is striking. In many island economies, tourism accounts for a large share of employment and foreign exchange. Hotels, taxis, guides, farmers, and artisans all depend on visitor flows. When arrivals drop, the effects ripple quickly. Governments are acutely aware of this dependence. It sharpens their sensitivity to reputational risk. It also sharpens their understanding of reputational value.

Tourism creates audiences. Visitors become informal ambassadors, carrying impressions home. Travel journalists and influencers mediate those impressions further. Rankings, awards, and listicles condense complex places into shorthand. Small states learn to work with these dynamics. They monitor coverage. They cultivate relationships. They intervene when narratives turn against them. The behaviour is reputation management. The consequence is not only bookings, but bargaining space.

The opening example of the polluted beach captures this logic. The threat was not legal sanction. It was reputational exposure. The government understood that the company's brand was vulnerable to scrutiny. The leverage lay in attention, not authority. By acting swiftly and visibly, the state signalled that environmental standards were non-negotiable. The clean-up restored more than sand. It reinforced a message about stewardship that resonated with visitors and partners alike.

This sensitivity to image extends beyond crisis response. Small states stage culture deliberately for global audiences. Festivals, music, sport, and cuisine travel well. They offer entry points into stories about place. Governments support these expressions not only for domestic pride, but for foreign policy effect. A film shot on location can do more to embed an island in public imagination than a decade of formal outreach.

The tension between authenticity and marketability is constant. Culture curated too heavily loses credibility. Culture left entirely to chance may fail to travel. Small states navigate this tension pragmatically. They invest in platforms rather than scripts, enabling artists and athletes to represent place on their own terms while ensuring visibility aligns with broader goals. The result is not uniform branding, but recognisable association.

A case from the Caribbean illustrates this balance. When a major film production chose to shoot across several islands in the early 2000s, governments competed quietly to attract scenes. They offered logistical support, streamlined permits, and promotional partnerships. The immediate gain was employment and exposure. The longer-term gain emerged in negotiations with airlines and cruise operators, who now recognised demand tied to familiar imagery.

Transport links improved. Tourism diversified. Cultural visibility translated into infrastructure leverage.

Hosting summits and high-level visits operates on a similar principle. Small states rarely dominate agendas in large capitals. By hosting, they invert the geography of attention. Leaders arrive on their terms, follow their schedules, and encounter issues framed by local context. Informal settings matter. Conversations over meals, walks along the coast, or boat trips create space for topics that struggle to surface in formal halls.

The costs are real. Security, logistics, accommodation, and staffing strain small administrations. Yet the returns can be disproportionate. A routine regional meeting becomes an opportunity to foreground concerns that might otherwise be marginal. A maritime security issue discussed while overlooking shipping lanes acquires immediacy. Place becomes argument.

Visibility itself becomes negotiating capital. Rankings for sustainability, safety, or visitor satisfaction circulate widely. Small states court them carefully. A favourable ranking attracts tourists, investors, and partners. It also creates leverage in discussions with airlines, development banks, and donors. Poor rankings prompt action. Leaders track these metrics not as vanity, but as instruments.

This logic explains why diplomats increasingly engage travel media alongside traditional counterparts. An ambassador arranging briefings for journalists is not indulging publicity for its own sake. They are shaping the environment in which negotiations occur. Positive coverage in a source market can soften resistance to climate financing or development cooperation. Negative coverage can stiffen it. The boundary between tourism promotion and diplomacy blurs.

A vignette captures this practice. In a European capital, an island ambassador hosts a reception timed to coincide with a tourism roadshow. Alongside chefs and musicians, the programme includes a short presentation on climate impacts. The message is subtle. Visitors drawn by beaches are invited to consider their fragility. The ambassador does not ask for commitments. The pairing lingers. Weeks later, in a separate policy meeting, the context is already set.

Soft power operates through accumulation. Individual acts matter less than patterns. Consistent messaging across tourism campaigns, cultural events, and diplomatic engagements builds a narrative of place. For small states, that narrative is often about stewardship, openness, and resilience. It distinguishes them in crowded markets and crowded forums alike.

Modern relevance sharpens the stakes. Social media accelerates reputational swings. A single incident can dominate feeds globally within hours. At the same time, platforms offer unprecedented reach for those who manage them well. Small states adapt quickly, often outpacing larger bureaucracies. They respond in real time, correct inaccuracies, and amplify positive stories. Agility becomes an asset.

The chapter also recognises limits. Tourism dependence can constrain criticism of powerful partners. Governments may hesitate to offend airlines, cruise lines, or source countries. Soft power cuts both ways. Visibility invites scrutiny. Small states navigate these risks by diversifying markets, investing in domestic capacity, and aligning tourism narratives with policy priorities rather than subordinating one to the other.

A recurring image threads through the chapter: the stage. Small states do not control the audience, but they can shape the performance. They choose what to light, what to leave in shadow, and when to change scenes. Tourism provides the stage. Culture supplies the script. Diplomacy manages the timing.

The closing movement of this introduction turns on a simple question. When attention itself becomes a currency, who spends it best? This chapter follows the governments and diplomats who understand that visibility, carefully handled, can substitute for size. It traces how beaches, festivals, summits, and headlines become tools of statecraft. Not as spectacle, but as strategy.

What follows is not a celebration of branding for its own sake. It is an examination of how small states live with exposure and turn it, at critical moments, into leverage. The reader is invited to see tourism not as a backdrop to diplomacy, but as one of its most dynamic arenas—where reputation is negotiated daily, and influence is earned in full view.

Tourism dependent island economies

In April 2020, when international flights stopped arriving at Grantley Adams International Airport in Barbados, the silence carried a measurable cost. Visitor arrivals fell by more than 70 per cent that year, according to the Barbados Statistical Service's 2021 tourism review. Hotels closed within weeks. Taxi drivers parked their cars indefinitely. Government revenue contracted sharply just as health spending rose. For an economy built around welcome, absence proved catastrophic. Tourism, long treated as a renewable asset, revealed itself as acutely fragile.

Dependence can look like strength until it does not.

The central argument of this section is that tourism dependence in small island economies is neither a simple vulnerability nor a passive condition. It is a structural exposure that magnifies external shocks, yet it also generates leverage precisely because it operates in the realm of reputation, visibility, and choice. States that understand this duality can convert dependence into bargaining power, not by denying fragility, but by managing attention.

Observation anchors the claim. In many island states, tourism accounts for a substantial share of employment and foreign exchange earnings. This concentration creates efficiency. Infrastructure, skills, and services align around a clear demand. The name for this configuration is sectoral focus. The explanation lies in comparative advantage: climate, geography, and culture attract visitors more readily than heavy industry ever could. The consequence is growth that is fast but uneven.

The same focus imports risk. Airlines, tour operators, cruise companies, and digital platforms mediate access to markets. Decisions made in distant boardrooms ripple quickly through local economies. A route cut, a ship redeployed, an algorithm adjusted—each can alter livelihoods overnight. External shocks compound the problem. Financial crises, pandemics, security scares, and extreme weather interrupt flows with little warning. The abstraction is exposure. The consequence is volatility borne locally.

This volatility has political weight. When tourism falters, unemployment rises quickly. Governments face pressure to subsidise wages, support businesses, and stabilise revenue. Fiscal buffers thin. Social cohesion strains. Dependence becomes visible not as an economic statistic but as a lived experience. Policymakers absorb the lesson early: reputation matters because demand is discretionary.

Yet discretion cuts both ways. Visitors choose destinations. Companies choose where to operate. That choice creates leverage for those who host. Tourism functions within a reputational marketplace where image, trust, and standards matter. Small states that recognise this can influence behaviour without resorting to blunt regulation.

A case from Southeast Asia illustrates this dynamic. In 2018, Thailand's government temporarily closed Maya Bay, made famous by the film *The Beach*, after environmental damage from overtourism became undeniable. The decision drew global attention. Operators protested. Visitors complained. Yet the closure reinforced Thailand's environmental credibility. When the bay reopened in 2022 under stricter rules, the message was clear: access was conditional. Reputation had been used to reset terms.

Island states apply similar logic on a smaller scale. The earlier example of a polluted beach demonstrates how reputational threat can discipline corporate behaviour. The government did not need to litigate. It signalled willingness to expose negligence to an audience that cared deeply about pristine imagery. The behaviour was reputational signalling. The explanation lay in asymmetry of risk: a negative story hurt the company more than the state. The consequence was rapid compliance.

Tourism dependence also sharpens regulatory strategy. Small states rarely compete on volume alone. They differentiate on quality, sustainability, and experience. Environmental standards, labour practices, and community engagement become part of the brand. Governments enforce selectively but visibly, knowing that enforcement itself communicates values. The abstraction is signalling through standards. The consequence is attraction of partners aligned with those values.

A second named example clarifies this approach. In 2019, Palau introduced its "Palau Pledge," requiring visitors to sign a commitment to respect the environment upon arrival. The initiative, backed by the Palau Visitors Authority, attracted international coverage. While largely symbolic, it reinforced Palau's positioning as a steward of marine ecosystems. According to the World Tourism Organization's 2020 commentary, the pledge enhanced the country's profile among environmentally conscious travellers. Symbol became strategy.

Tourism dependence also shapes diplomatic posture. States mindful of their image invest in crisis response capacity. When incidents occur—accidents, crimes, environmental damage—governments respond swiftly and publicly. Silence invites speculation. Transparency reassures. The behaviour is narrative control. The explanation lies in information velocity. The consequence is damage containment.

Airlines illustrate another leverage point. Route decisions are commercial, but they are sensitive to demand signals and policy environments. Small states negotiate incentives, marketing partnerships, and infrastructure support to attract or retain routes. They also coordinate diplomatically when routes are threatened. Tourism boards and foreign ministries collaborate. The abstraction is market shaping. The consequence is connectivity preserved.

Cruise tourism adds complexity. Cruise lines deliver volume but capture much of the value offshore.

Environmental and social impacts concentrate locally. Island governments face difficult trade-offs: restrict access and risk retaliation, or accept costs to sustain flows. Some have begun to assert standards more forcefully. In Venice, though not an island state in the same sense, the 2021 ban on large cruise ships through the Giudecca Canal signalled a broader shift. Image and heritage justified constraint.

Small island economies observe these precedents closely. They learn that saying no can sometimes increase leverage. Scarcity can be an asset. Exclusivity, when credible, raises value. The behaviour is controlled access. The explanation lies in demand elasticity among certain market segments. The consequence is bargaining power regained.

There is, however, a credible limitation. Tourism dependence constrains criticism of major source markets. Governments may hesitate to confront countries whose citizens constitute large shares of arrivals. Diplomatic positions can soften. Environmental enforcement can waver. This risk of capture is real.

Reconciling the limitation requires diversification. Successful states spread source markets, encourage longer stays, and develop complementary sectors such as education or specialised services. Diversification does not eliminate dependence; it reduces vulnerability to any single shock. The abstraction is portfolio management. The consequence is resilience through balance.

Observable behaviours mark this shift. Marketing campaigns target new regions. Visa regimes adjust. Niche tourism—diving, wellness, conferences—expands. Each step broadens the base without abandoning the core. Governments track metrics such as average spend per visitor and length of stay, not just arrivals. Quality supplants quantity as the guiding measure.

The motif binding this section is the lens. Tourism is the lens through which the world sees small island states. That lens can distort or clarify. Governments that polish it obsessively miss substance. Governments that ignore it invite misrepresentation. The art lies in calibration.

The lens appears again in political leverage. When environmental damage threatens the image, states act decisively. When labour abuses surface, they intervene. Each intervention reinforces the message that access is conditional on respect. Over time, this consistency builds a reputation that itself deters misconduct.

The closing choice is sharpened. Treat tourism dependence as a trap that limits agency, or treat it as a stage on which agency can be exercised. Small island economies cannot wish away dependence. They can decide how to inhabit it. Those that understand the politics of attention, and act accordingly, find that even fragile industries can yield leverage when reputation is guarded as carefully as revenue.

Staging culture for global audiences

In June 2019, when the film *No Time to Die* premiered its Jamaica-shot sequences, the island appeared on cinema screens worldwide as a place of striking colour, motion, and coastal drama. Long before audiences noticed the scenery, officials had been negotiating the production's logistics with studios and insurers. The numbers were concrete. According to Jamaica Promotions Corporation figures released in 2020, the film injected tens of millions of dollars into the local economy during production. Less visible, but more enduring, were the conversations that followed with airlines and tour operators, who now had fresh imagery to sell and renewed incentive to expand routes. Culture had travelled ahead of policy.

Images cross borders faster than communiqués.

The thesis of this section is that culture, when staged with intention, functions as a durable instrument of foreign policy for small states. Festivals, music, sport, cuisine, and film do not merely entertain; they shape public opinion, condition demand, and open diplomatic space in markets that formal diplomacy reaches only intermittently. The challenge lies in balancing authenticity with marketability, avoiding both caricature and obscurity. Small states that manage this balance convert cultural visibility into tangible negotiating capital.

Observation grounds the claim. In global consciousness, many island states are known first through cultural shorthand. A rhythm. A dish. A sporting hero. A film location. These impressions precede policy positions and colour receptivity to them. The name for this phenomenon is pre-attentive framing. The explanation lies in how audiences process distant places. The consequence is that culture sets the terms on which later messages are received.

Cultural festivals illustrate the mechanism clearly. Carnivals, music festivals, and culinary events draw international visitors and media attention. They compress complex histories into sensory experience. Governments support these events not simply for tourism revenue, but because they anchor national narratives in recognisable forms. The behaviour is narrative condensation. The explanation lies in attention economics. The consequence is a platform from which broader stories can be told.

Consider the Trinidad and Tobago Carnival. Its global reputation rests on decades of artistic labour, not state scripting. Yet public institutions have learned to align with it strategically. Diplomatic missions host related events abroad. Tourism campaigns synchronise with festival cycles. According to UNESCO's 2021 recognition of Carnival traditions as intangible cultural heritage, such acknowledgment amplifies international visibility. Culture here operates as a bridge between local practice and global recognition.

Music travels even further. Genres associated with island states—reggae, calypso, soca—carry political resonance alongside sound. Artists become informal envoys. Their lyrics, aesthetics, and affiliations shape perceptions of place. Governments cannot control this flow, nor should they. What they can do is support infrastructure that allows cultural production to flourish and circulate. The abstraction is enabling environment. The consequence is soft power that feels organic rather than imposed.

Sport offers a different vector. When a sprinter from Jamaica or a cricketer from a small Caribbean state dominates international competition, national identity becomes visible in arenas otherwise indifferent to geography. Sporting success compresses narratives of discipline, excellence, and possibility into singular moments. Governments invest in sport partly for domestic reasons, but the external effects are substantial. Visibility attracts interest. Interest invites engagement.

Cuisine completes the quartet. Food is intimate, repeatable, and social. Restaurants abroad function as informal embassies. Ingredients carry supply chains. Culinary festivals attract media. When an island cuisine gains prominence, it alters expectations about quality and sophistication. The behaviour is taste diplomacy. The explanation lies in embodied experience. The consequence is affinity that outlasts campaigns.

The tension between authenticity and marketability runs through all these domains. Culture tailored too explicitly for external consumption risks dilution. Culture left entirely inward-facing may fail to travel. Small states navigate this tension pragmatically. They curate context rather than content. They allow artists, chefs, and athletes to speak in their own voices while ensuring platforms exist for those voices to be heard.

The film production example from Jamaica sharpens this point. The government did not script the narrative. It facilitated access. It ensured that landscapes, labour, and logistics were available. The result was imagery that felt authentic because it was not overtly promotional. Yet its impact on transport negotiations was unmistakable. Airlines capitalised on renewed interest. Discussions about route expansion gained momentum. Culture had altered the bargaining environment.

A second named example reinforces the pattern. New Zealand's engagement with the *Lord of the Rings* film trilogy in the early 2000s transformed the country's global image. According to Tourism New Zealand reports from 2004 onward, visitor interest surged, and the "100% Pure New Zealand" campaign integrated cinematic landscapes into broader branding. While New Zealand is not a microstate, the lesson scales down. Strategic facilitation of cultural production can yield diplomatic dividends.

The behaviours involved are subtle. Governments offer tax incentives, streamline permits, and coordinate agencies. They avoid heavy-handed branding during production, allowing cultural products to breathe. The explanation lies in credibility preservation. The consequence is imagery that audiences trust.

A credible limitation must be acknowledged. Cultural staging can reinforce stereotypes. Islands risk being reduced to scenery or spectacle. When this happens, political agency can be obscured rather than enhanced. Visitors consume images without engaging realities.

Reconciling this limitation requires diversification of cultural narratives. Small states increasingly showcase contemporary art, innovation, and social debate alongside traditional motifs. Film festivals, design weeks, and literary events broaden the frame. The abstraction is narrative pluralism. The consequence is a more complex, resilient image of place.

Metrics help guide these choices. Media sentiment analysis. Audience reach. Duration of coverage. Governments track not just volume of attention, but its quality. They ask whether coverage associates the country with competence, creativity, and stewardship. These attributes matter when negotiating beyond tourism.

The motif binding this section is the stage. Culture is staged not in the sense of artificiality, but of presentation. Lighting, framing, and timing matter. Small states do not control the script entirely, but they decide which stages to build and which performances to support. The stage appears again when cultural events are hosted abroad, creating temporary islands of attention in foreign cities.

Modern relevance intensifies the argument. Digital platforms accelerate cultural diffusion. A music video filmed on an island can reach millions overnight. A cooking clip can spark curiosity far from traditional markets. Small states adapt quickly, often with limited resources but high agility. They collaborate with creators rather than command them. They understand that authenticity travels faster than polish.

The section closes on a sharpened choice. Treat culture as ornament, or treat it as infrastructure for influence. Small states that invest in cultural ecosystems—rather than slogans—find that global audiences become more receptive partners. Staging culture well does not guarantee favourable outcomes. It shapes the room in which outcomes are negotiated, enlarging the space in which small voices can be heard without shouting.

Hosting summits and high level visits

On 3 September 2018, leaders from across the Pacific gathered in Nauru for the forty-ninth Pacific Islands Forum. The meeting itself followed a familiar pattern of speeches and communiqués. The setting did not. Delegates arrived by chartered aircraft to a coral atoll barely twenty-one square kilometres in size, its single road circling the island, its phosphate-scarred interior visible from the air. Security convoys were short. Distances were walkable. Conversations spilled from meeting rooms into shaded outdoor spaces where the sea was always within sight. By the end of the week, maritime security and illegal fishing dominated the agenda. Place had done part of the work.

Hosting rearranges attention.

The central argument of this section is that when small states host summits and high-level visits, they gain a form of procedural and spatial leverage unavailable in larger capitals. Control over venues, schedules, and informal spaces allows hosts to shape not only what is discussed, but how it is discussed. The effect is subtle, cumulative, and often underestimated. At the same time, hosting imposes heavy logistical and financial burdens that can strain small administrations. The decision to host is therefore strategic rather than ceremonial.

Observation grounds the claim. In most diplomatic settings, small states arrive as guests. Agendas are set elsewhere. Time is rationed. Informal access is limited. Hosting inverts this dynamic. The host decides where meetings take place, how days are structured, and which issues are woven into social events. The name for this advantage is agenda adjacency. The explanation lies in proximity and repetition. The consequence is greater influence over emphasis, tone, and sequencing.

Venues matter more than is often acknowledged. A conference hall overlooking shipping lanes invites different discussion from one buried in a capital's financial district. A retreat setting encourages candour. Seating arrangements shape who speaks to whom. Small states use these tools deliberately. They select venues that embody their priorities, whether environmental vulnerability, maritime exposure, or cultural heritage. The abstraction is spatial signalling. The consequence is context that reinforces message.

Schedules exert similar influence. Hosts determine pacing. They can cluster related sessions, extend breaks where informal discussion is valuable, or compress topics they wish to downplay. This is not manipulation; it is design. The behaviour is temporal framing. The explanation lies in cognitive load. The consequence is focus where the host prefers it.

Informal spaces complete the triad. Meals, excursions, and cultural performances provide opportunities to surface issues that struggle in plenary sessions. Small states excel here because scale reduces formality. Ministers encounter one another repeatedly. Conversations resume easily. Trust builds faster. The abstraction is social density. The consequence is accelerated relationship formation.

The Nauru Forum illustrates these dynamics. Maritime security had been discussed before. What changed was its salience. Delegates could not ignore the sea that sustained and threatened the host. Illegal fishing, transnational crime, and climate-related displacement became tangible rather than abstract. According to the Forum's 2018 communiqué, commitments on maritime cooperation were strengthened. Hosting had altered the conversational centre of gravity.

A second example reinforces the point. In 2014, Seychelles hosted the Indian Ocean Rim Association Leaders' Summit. For Seychelles, maritime security and the blue economy were existential concerns. By hosting, it placed these issues at the heart of proceedings. Side events showcased marine conservation projects. Informal discussions focused on piracy and fisheries management. The final declaration reflected these priorities more clearly than previous meetings, according to IORA documentation that year. The host's interests had become collective language.

These outcomes are not accidental. Foreign ministries plan meticulously. They coordinate across agencies. They brief domestic stakeholders. They anticipate sensitivities. Hosting becomes a project that mobilises the state. The behaviour is whole-of-government engagement. The explanation lies in concentrated opportunity. The consequence is coherence rarely achievable in dispersed diplomacy.

The burdens are significant. Security costs escalate. Infrastructure must meet international standards. Staff work extended hours for months. Budgets stretch. For microstates, a single summit can absorb a large share of annual discretionary spending. This is the credible limitation of hosting as leverage.

Reconciling the limitation requires selectivity. Small states host fewer events, but extract more from them. They choose meetings aligned closely with strategic priorities. They seek cost-sharing arrangements. They leverage regional organisations for support. The behaviour is strategic scarcity. The explanation lies in capacity management. The consequence is sustainability.

Observable metrics guide these decisions. Number of bilateral meetings held on the margins. References to host priorities in final texts. Follow-up initiatives launched. Hosts evaluate success not by applause, but by uptake. Did partners commit resources? Did language shift? Did relationships deepen?

High-level visits operate on a similar logic, though at smaller scale. When a head of government visits a microstate, the visit is often immersive. Distances are short. Media coverage is concentrated. Hosts curate programmes carefully, exposing visitors to specific realities. A visit to a coastal village, a patrol vessel, or a research centre communicates priorities more forcefully than briefing papers.

A case sketch illustrates this practice. During a routine regional summit hosted by a Caribbean island in the late 2010s, the foreign ministry arranged an early-morning boat trip for visiting ministers to observe shipping traffic near a congested strait. The trip was brief. The visual impact was lasting. Later that day, maritime security featured prominently in discussions that might otherwise have focused on trade. The host had transformed a routine meeting into a demonstration.

The motif binding this section is the table. Hosting determines who sits where, who pours the coffee, who sets the pace. The table is physical and symbolic. Those who set it influence the conversation that unfolds upon it. The motif appears again when small states host retreats where seating is circular rather than hierarchical, subtly altering interaction.

Modern relevance heightens the stakes. Virtual meetings have proliferated, reducing the frequency of in-person summits. When they do occur, their impact is magnified. Hosting becomes rarer and more valuable. Small states that host well stand out. They offer experiences that cannot be replicated on screens.

There is also reputational risk. Poorly organised events damage credibility. Security lapses draw scrutiny. Small states mitigate these risks through partnerships with regional bodies and experienced contractors. They learn quickly. Each hosted event builds institutional memory.

Hosting does not guarantee influence. Delegates arrive with fixed positions. Power asymmetries remain. Yet hosting changes the texture of interaction. It creates moments where listening precedes asserting. For small states, these moments matter.

The section closes on a sharpened choice. Decline hosting to conserve resources, or host selectively to shape agendas that would otherwise marginalise vital concerns. Small states that choose the latter treat summits not as showcases, but as instruments. They understand that where diplomacy happens can matter as much as what is said. When place and purpose align, even routine meetings can be turned into platforms where small states briefly, but decisively, stand at the centre of wider conversations.

Turning visibility into negotiating capital

In July 2019, as a European heatwave pushed temperatures past forty degrees, a small island state appeared near the top of a widely circulated travel ranking for "cooler summer escapes." The list was compiled by a major media outlet and syndicated across platforms within days. Tourist enquiries spiked. More quietly, officials in the island's embassy in Berlin noted a change in tone during meetings with transport regulators and climate officials. The country had become visible in a way that was timely, flattering, and useful. Visibility, it turned out, had arrived carrying leverage.

Attention is not neutral currency.

The central claim of this section is that publicity, rankings, and media coverage constitute a form of negotiating capital for small states when handled deliberately. Visibility shapes reputations, conditions expectations, and alters the bargaining environment in which formal diplomacy takes place. Leaders who court travel journalists, editors, and influencers alongside diplomats do so not out of vanity, but because mediated attention reaches audiences and decision-makers that traditional diplomatic channels touch only intermittently. When visibility aligns with strategic objectives, it becomes convertible into favourable terms.

Observation grounds the argument. In a crowded international system, most small states struggle for notice. Their policy papers circulate narrowly. Their speeches compete for airtime. Yet travel features, lifestyle rankings, and cultural coverage travel widely and persistently. They enter homes, phones, and social feeds. The name for this phenomenon is asymmetrical reach. The explanation lies in audience appetite. The consequence is that non-political coverage can have political effects.

Rankings exemplify this dynamic. Lists of safest destinations, most sustainable beaches, or best value holidays condense complex assessments into digestible signals. They are blunt instruments, but influential ones. Governments track them closely. A rise can attract visitors and investors. A fall can prompt scrutiny. Small states learn to anticipate and, where possible, influence these signals through policy choices that align with ranking criteria.

This behaviour is not manipulation. It is calibration. When an island invests in marine protection, it does so for ecological reasons first. When that investment improves sustainability rankings, the reputational return amplifies the original decision. The abstraction is reputational yield. The consequence is increased interest from partners seeking association with positive narratives.

Media coverage operates similarly. Travel journalism has evolved beyond brochures. Investigative features on over-tourism, environmental degradation, or labour practices can shape demand quickly. Governments respond by engaging journalists proactively, offering access, data, and context. The behaviour is pre-emptive engagement. The explanation lies in narrative competition. The consequence is greater influence over framing.

A named example illustrates this craft. Iceland's tourism surge after the 2010 Eyjafjallajökull eruption prompted a sophisticated media strategy. While Iceland is larger than many microstates, the lesson resonates. The government and tourism bodies worked with journalists to highlight resilience, safety, and infrastructure. According to Visit Iceland's 2012 review, this approach helped convert disruption into curiosity. Visibility, even when sparked by crisis, became an asset.

Small island states apply similar logic at different scales. They invite journalists to see adaptation projects, not just beaches. They highlight local innovation. They respond quickly to inaccuracies. The behaviour is narrative stewardship. The explanation lies in trust-building. The consequence is coverage that supports rather than undermines policy goals.

Influencers add another layer. Their reach is narrower but more targeted. Governments engage selectively, aware that authenticity matters. Heavy-handed sponsorship backfires. Instead, states facilitate experiences aligned with values they wish to project—environmental care, cultural depth, safety. Influencers translate these experiences into personal stories that audiences trust. The abstraction is peer validation. The consequence is reputational reinforcement.

Visibility becomes negotiating capital when it alters counterpart incentives. Airlines consider routes to destinations with rising profiles. Development partners prefer association with positive stories. Investors respond to brand strength as a proxy for stability. Small states use this awareness to time negotiations, aligning proposals with peaks in favourable attention.

A vignette captures this strategy. In a northern European capital, an ambassador from a Caribbean island coordinated a tourism campaign highlighting coral restoration with a series of policy briefings on climate finance. The campaign ran across travel magazines and digital platforms. In meetings that followed, officials referenced the coverage unprompted. The ambassador did not argue for vulnerability. She pointed to visibility. The message was implicit: partnership here would be noticed.

The behaviour was coupling. The explanation lay in context creation. The consequence was receptivity that would have been harder to achieve in isolation.

Publicity also affects domestic bargaining power. Leaders leverage international praise to justify reforms at home. A high sustainability ranking strengthens arguments for environmental regulation. Positive coverage reassures citizens that sacrifices yield recognition. Visibility thus feeds back into political capacity.

There is, however, a credible limitation. Visibility attracts scrutiny. When narratives turn negative, leverage reverses.

Scandals amplify quickly. Small states lack the resources to absorb prolonged reputational damage. Dependence on attention can become dependency on approval.

Reconciling this limitation requires resilience in messaging. Successful states diversify narratives. They avoid tying reputation to a single claim or image. They invest in institutional transparency so that scrutiny, when it comes, finds substance. The abstraction is reputational depth. The consequence is durability.

Metrics guide this work. Governments monitor sentiment, not just volume. They distinguish between fleeting virality and sustained recognition. They track correlations between coverage and concrete outcomes: route announcements, partnership offers, policy invitations. Visibility without conversion is noise.

The motif binding this section is the mirror. Media reflects and distorts. Small states learn to adjust posture without losing form. They check how they appear, then decide what to change in reality rather than the reflection alone. The mirror appears again when leaders use rankings as diagnostics, not trophies.

Modern relevance intensifies the stakes. Algorithms reward novelty. Attention cycles shorten. Small states respond with agility. They maintain rapid-response teams. They coordinate across ministries. They accept that silence cedes narrative space.

The section closes on a sharpened choice. Treat visibility as decoration, or treat it as capital to be invested, protected, and spent judiciously. Small states that choose the latter understand that in an attention economy, influence often arrives before invitation. By shaping how they are seen, they shape the terms on which they are approached. Visibility, carefully handled, becomes not an end in itself, but a lever—lightweight, fragile, and capable of moving more than its size suggests.

Chapter 6
Diasporas as Hidden Embassies

On a weekday evening in October 2017, a modest church hall in outer London filled with voices carrying an accent rarely heard in Westminster. The gathering was not a cultural festival or a fundraising dinner. It was a briefing. Printed maps lay on folding tables, marking coastal villages and erosion lines. By the end of the night, attendees had divided tasks: who would contact which Member of Parliament, who would draft a short explainer for journalists, who would follow up with a think tank specialising in climate risk. The country in question was a microstate thousands of kilometres away. The influence being mobilised sat firmly inside one of Europe's most powerful capitals.

Embassies do not always fly flags.

Diasporas have long been discussed as sources of remittances or nostalgia, occasionally as political irritants. This chapter treats them differently. It approaches diasporas as dispersed diplomatic infrastructure—uneven, informal, and often underestimated. For small states with limited missions abroad, citizens and descendants living overseas extend the state's reach into places where formal embassies are thinly staffed or entirely absent. They listen, translate, advocate, and sometimes obstruct. Their power lies not in uniformity, but in density.

The paradox is clear. The further people move from the homeland, the closer they often sit to power.

Small states are marked by outward movement. Education, employment, and historical ties scatter citizens across global cities. These communities are not monolithic. They differ by generation, class, profession, and political outlook. Some maintain intense engagement with home affairs; others loosen ties deliberately. Treating diaspora as a single actor misreads its complexity. Yet within that diversity lie clusters of influence that small states can neither ignore nor fully command.

This chapter explores how those clusters function as hidden embassies. It traces the ways overseas communities form hubs in particular cities and sectors, how money and expertise flow back through family and professional networks, how diaspora voices operate in foreign legislatures and media, and how coordinated campaigns link mobilisation abroad with strategy at home. It also confronts the tensions: representation, legitimacy, and backlash.

Mapping overseas communities is the first act of this diplomacy, whether undertaken consciously or not. Small states learn quickly that their citizens abroad tend to concentrate geographically and occupationally. A microstate may have a modest presence in dozens of countries, but a dense cluster in one metropolitan region that matters disproportionately. Often these regions host international institutions, shipping centres, financial hubs, or legislative power. Presence becomes proximity.

Consulates, churches, alumni groups, sports clubs, and professional associations operate as informal listening posts. Information flows through them faster than through official channels. They register shifts in mood, policy debates, and personnel changes. For understaffed foreign ministries, these signals are invaluable. The diaspora does not replace formal diplomacy. It supplements it with texture and speed.

The political significance of remittances is well known, though often discussed only in economic terms. Money sent home supports families, stabilises consumption, and cushions shocks. In many small states, these flows rival or exceed official development assistance. Yet remittances are only the most visible part of a broader exchange. Ideas, expectations, and practices travel with equal force.

Diaspora professionals act as brokers. Engineers advise on infrastructure projects. Lawyers interpret regulatory shifts. Academics connect universities. Business leaders identify market opportunities. Much of this activity is quiet, undocumented, and driven by personal loyalty rather than policy instruction. Its cumulative effect, however, is substantial. Capability migrates outward and then circulates back in fragments.

A shipping executive steering new routes towards their ancestral port, or facilitating training placements for young officers, rarely appears in diplomatic reporting. The impact is nonetheless strategic. Trade patterns shift. Skills deepen. The state benefits without issuing a communiqué. Influence accrues sideways.

Diaspora voices in foreign capitals operate in more overtly political spaces. Community leaders brief legislators, contribute to media debates, and appear in policy forums. They translate home concerns into the idiom of host countries, framing them in terms that resonate locally: security, jobs, climate risk, moral responsibility. When coordinated with embassies, this amplification can be decisive. When uncoordinated, it can confuse or undermine official positions.

The risk of backlash is real. Diaspora advocacy can provoke accusations of dual loyalty or foreign interference. Small states must therefore tread carefully. Effective engagement relies on alignment rather than instruction, mutual respect rather than control. Embassies that treat diaspora actors as instruments often lose them. Those that treat them as partners tend to gain discretion and trust.

Coordinated campaigns reveal the full potential and fragility of diaspora diplomacy. Petitions, rallies, social media actions, and targeted outreach can converge around key moments: a parliamentary vote, a budget decision, a multilateral negotiation. When synchronised with official lobbying, such campaigns extend reach and multiply pressure. When misaligned, they dilute messages and exhaust goodwill.

The image threading this chapter is that of a network rather than a hierarchy. Diasporas do not report up a chain of command. They operate through nodes and links, intensifying around shared moments and then dispersing. Small states that understand this logic stop trying to centralise and start learning to connect.

Modern relevance sharpens the stakes. Migration has accelerated. Digital platforms allow constant contact across borders. Political mobilisation travels quickly and unpredictably. For small states facing climate threats, debt negotiations, or security challenges, diaspora engagement is no longer optional background noise. It is part of the strategic environment.

This chapter does not romanticise diaspora power. It examines its limits, its internal divisions, and its ethical complications. Representation is contested. Accountability is uneven. Voices abroad can diverge sharply from realities at home. Yet ignoring this field leaves influence untapped and narratives unchallenged.

What follows traces the mechanics of diaspora diplomacy with precision and restraint. It shows how small states map their overseas communities, convert social ties into economic and political influence, manage advocacy in foreign capitals, and orchestrate campaigns that link the street corner to the negotiating table. The aim is not to celebrate reach for its own sake, but to understand how dispersed people become part of statecraft.

The reader is invited to see embassies differently after this chapter—not only as buildings with plaques, but as living networks of citizens who, intentionally or not, extend the state's presence far beyond its borders.

Mapping overseas communities and hubs

In March 2015, a small consular office in Geneva quietly updated its contact list after noticing a pattern. Over the previous year, an unusual number of calls and emails had come from the same handful of postcodes. The callers worked at shipping firms, environmental NGOs, and international organisations clustered along the lake. They shared a birthplace: a Pacific microstate with no permanent mission to the United Nations offices nearby. According to Swiss federal statistics released in 2014, fewer than three thousand citizens from that country lived in Switzerland. Yet within walking distance of Palais des Nations, their presence was dense enough to matter.

Diaspora influence is rarely proportional to headcount.

The core argument of this section is that overseas communities from small states do not disperse evenly. They cluster—by city, by sector, by institution—and those clusters function as informal extensions of the state's diplomatic reach. Understanding diaspora influence therefore begins not with aggregate numbers, but with mapping: identifying where people concentrate, what they do, and how they connect. For small states with limited embassies and thin staffing, this mapping becomes a form of strategic intelligence.

Observation grounds the claim. Migration from small states follows pathways shaped by education systems, colonial legacies, labour markets, and visa regimes. Engineers gravitate to infrastructure hubs. Lawyers to regulatory centres. Seafarers to ports. Students to universities that replicate themselves through alumni networks. The name for this pattern is selective concentration. The explanation lies in opportunity structures rather than sentiment. The consequence is that influence accumulates in specific places, not everywhere at once.

This concentration produces hubs. A diaspora hub is not simply a neighbourhood. It is a dense intersection of people, institutions, and routines. Hubs emerge in global cities that host decision-making power: capitals, financial centres, shipping crossroads, and international organisations. A microstate may have a handful of citizens scattered across a country, but a critical mass in one metropolitan area that shapes outcomes far beyond its size.

Diversity within diaspora communities complicates this picture. Overseas citizens differ by generation, class, political orientation, and degree of attachment to home. Some retain voting rights and follow domestic politics closely. Others define themselves primarily through professional identity. Loyalty is not uniform. Capacity is uneven. Treating diaspora as a single actor flattens this reality and invites miscalculation.

Effective mapping therefore distinguishes between layers. Long-settled communities often provide stability and institutional memory. Recent migrants bring energy and current knowledge. Students supply networks that will mature later. Professionals embedded in key sectors offer access. Each layer contributes differently. The abstraction is heterogeneity. The consequence is that engagement strategies must vary.

Consulates, churches, and associations emerge as anchor points within this landscape. They provide continuity amid turnover. A church congregation may gather weekly for decades, sustaining ties across generations. Professional associations organise around shared practice rather than nationality, yet often become spaces where compatriots find one another. Consulates, even when understaffed, serve as symbolic centres where information converges.

These institutions act as informal listening posts. They register shifts in sentiment, track policy debates in host countries, and surface opportunities before they reach formal channels. A consular officer hears concerns about visa changes at a community event. A pastor learns of labour disputes affecting migrants. An alumni group flags a funding call at a university. The behaviour is ambient monitoring. The explanation lies in proximity to everyday life. The consequence is early warning.

A concrete example illustrates this function. Citizens of the Marshall Islands have formed a notable community in Arkansas, drawn by employment opportunities and educational pathways under the Compact of Free Association with the United States. According to the U.S. Census Bureau's American Community Survey in 2019, Arkansas hosts one of the largest Marshallese populations outside the Pacific. Churches in Springdale became centres not only of worship, but of political organisation and information exchange. When health and labour issues affecting the community emerged, these networks connected local experience to national advocacy. Density translated into voice.

A different pattern appears in Europe. The diaspora of Malta, though small numerically, concentrates in Brussels and Strasbourg due to EU institutions. Maltese nationals working as civil servants, advisers, and interns form overlapping networks that interact daily with policy processes. The Maltese Permanent Representation benefits from this proximity, gaining insight into informal debates and personnel changes. According to EU staff directories published in 2018, Maltese nationals are overrepresented relative to population size in certain administrative units. Mapping revealed leverage invisible in headline statistics.

These examples underscore a key point. Influence flows from where people are positioned, not merely from how many there are. A single diaspora hub embedded in a strategic sector can outweigh thousands dispersed elsewhere. Mapping seeks these points of density.

Observable behaviours mark successful mapping efforts. Foreign ministries maintain updated registries beyond passport lists, noting professions and affiliations. They attend community events not for ceremony, but for listening. They cross-reference migration data with institutional maps: where are international organisations headquartered, where are major ports, where do regulatory decisions cluster? The abstraction is situational awareness. The consequence is targeted engagement.

Technology has sharpened this process. Social media groups, professional platforms, and messaging apps reveal patterns of interaction. Governments that monitor these spaces ethically and transparently gain insight into emerging hubs. Those that rely solely on formal registration lag behind reality. Mapping becomes iterative rather than static.

There is a credible limitation. Over-mapping can slide into surveillance, eroding trust. Diaspora communities may resist engagement if they feel instrumentalised or monitored. Small states, whose relationships with citizens are often intimate, must tread carefully.

Reconciling this limitation requires consent and reciprocity. Successful mapping is participatory. Governments explain why information matters and how it will be used. They offer services in return: support for community initiatives, access to officials, platforms for dialogue. The behaviour is trust-building. The explanation lies in mutual benefit. The consequence is sustained cooperation.

The motif binding this section is the map itself—not as a static chart, but as a living document. Routes shift. Hubs rise and fade. New sectors emerge. Mapping must be continuous. The map appears again when a crisis hits and governments need to know whom to call, where to convene, and which channels carry weight.

Modern relevance intensifies this need. Migration patterns change rapidly. Climate displacement, remote work, and geopolitical shifts alter where citizens settle. A diaspora hub today may not exist in ten years. Small states that update their maps remain agile. Those that cling to outdated assumptions lose reach.

Mapping also reveals gaps. Certain regions or sectors may lack diaspora presence, leaving blind spots. Recognising absence is as important as recognising density. It guides decisions about where to open honorary consulates, where to invest in scholarships, or where to deploy cultural diplomacy to seed future networks.

The section closes on a sharpened test. When a policy issue arises in a foreign capital, can a small state identify, within hours, who among its overseas community understands the issue, has access to relevant spaces, and is willing to engage? If the answer is yes, mapping has succeeded. If not, influence remains latent.

Diasporas do not automatically function as hidden embassies. They become so when states learn where they are, who they include, and how they connect. Mapping is the first discipline of that learning—a quiet, patient practice that turns scattered lives into strategic presence without denying their diversity or autonomy.

Remittances, business ties and influence

In 2022 the World Bank estimated that remittances to low- and middle-income countries reached roughly US$647 billion, exceeding official development assistance by a wide margin in the same year (World Bank, 2023). That figure is often cited in aggregate, but its meaning sharpens when narrowed to small states. In Port Vila, Vanuatu, on a humid afternoon in August 2021, a local bank manager described how monthly transfers from relatives in Australia and New Zealand kept construction firms solvent after border closures froze tourism. The air smelled of damp concrete and diesel. Aid programmes were discussed in press releases. Remittances arrived quietly, line by line.

Money moves faster than policy.

The central claim of this section is that remittances and diaspora business ties are not merely economic lifelines; they are instruments of influence that reshape bargaining power, institutional capacity, and strategic choice in small states. These flows carry cash, but also expectations, standards, and access. When understood as a system rather than as charity, they alter how small states negotiate with partners at home and abroad.

Observation comes first. For many microstates, money sent home by citizens abroad regularly surpasses inflows from bilateral aid programmes. This is not a marginal supplement. It is a structural feature of the economy. The name for this pattern is private external finance. The explanation lies in labour mobility and wage differentials: even modest earnings abroad translate into significant purchasing power at home. The consequence is fiscal breathing space that sits outside government budgets.

This breathing space has political effects. Families supported by remittances rely less on state transfers. Governments facing budget constraints know that certain social pressures are cushioned by private flows. This can stabilise societies during shocks, as seen after cyclones or commodity price swings. It can also mask vulnerability, allowing structural weaknesses to persist. Influence emerges in this tension.

The abstraction of remittances often obscures behaviour. Money is sent for specific reasons: school fees, medical bills, housing repairs. These uses shape priorities. A steady stream of tuition payments creates demand for local schools and scholarships. Health-related transfers expose gaps in domestic care. Housing remittances inflate land values. Each transaction signals where institutions fail or succeed. Policymakers who read these signals gain insight unavailable in macroeconomic tables.

A named example clarifies the dynamic. Tonga has long relied on overseas labour, particularly in New Zealand, Australia, and the United States. According to the Reserve Bank of Tonga's annual report for 2019, remittances accounted for a substantial share of foreign exchange earnings. During the COVID-19 border closures, these flows dipped briefly, then rebounded as diaspora communities mobilised support. The rebound did more than stabilise consumption. It funded small businesses and church-led welfare programmes that filled gaps left by the state. Influence flowed from private initiative.

Beyond cash, diaspora business ties transmit ideas and opportunities. Professionals abroad broker introductions, translate regulatory expectations, and reduce uncertainty for investors. The name for this function is relational capital. The explanation lies in trust: shared origin lowers perceived risk. The consequence is access.

Shipping offers a telling case. In 2017, a senior executive of a European shipping line, born in a Caribbean island state, began informal conversations with port authorities in his ancestral home. No memorandum announced the talks. Over two years, he facilitated training placements for local cadets, advised on port efficiency standards, and quietly adjusted routing discussions to include a trial call at the island's main harbour. The place was Rotterdam; the dates spanned 2017–2019. The result was a modest but durable increase in connectivity that no trade mission had secured. The behaviour was brokerage. The explanation lay in credibility on both sides. The consequence was structural.

Such cases repeat across sectors. Diaspora engineers advise on grid upgrades. Doctors organise visiting clinics. Academics arrange joint research bids. Each instance looks small. Together, they accumulate into influence. They shape which projects move first, which partners are trusted, which standards become normal.

Observable metrics capture this accumulation imperfectly. Counts of foreign direct investment miss advisory roles. Aid statistics ignore unpaid expertise. Yet ministries notice patterns: repeated offers of help from the same networks, recurring names in project pipelines. Mapping these patterns reveals leverage points.

A second named example comes from Mauritius. The country has cultivated ties with its diaspora in finance and technology hubs. According to a report by the Economic Development Board of Mauritius in 2020, diaspora professionals played a role in attracting fintech firms and structuring regulatory frameworks that balanced innovation with compliance. These were not mass remittance flows. They were targeted interventions that shaped policy design. Influence arrived as code and clauses, not cheques.

There is a credible limitation. Remittances can entrench dependency and inequality. Households without overseas relatives fall behind. Consumption-driven transfers may inflate prices without boosting productivity. Governments may delay reform, relying on private flows as a buffer. Influence, in this sense, can distort incentives.

Reconciling this limitation requires clarity. States that treat remittances as substitutes for policy abdicate responsibility.

Those that integrate them into planning—by reducing transfer costs, encouraging productive use, and aligning diaspora expertise with national priorities—convert private flows into public goods. The behaviour shifts from passive receipt to active coordination. The consequence is balance.

Ideas flow alongside money. Diaspora professionals carry norms from host countries: procurement standards, safety expectations, governance practices. When they advise at home, these norms travel. Sometimes they clash with local realities. Sometimes they catalyse reform. The abstraction is norm diffusion. The explanation lies in repeated exposure. The consequence is gradual institutional change.

The motif threading this section is circulation. Money circulates. Skills circulate. Influence circulates. Unlike aid, which often moves in one direction on fixed terms, diaspora flows loop. They respond to conditions. They accelerate when trust grows and slow when confidence erodes. Understanding this circulation allows small states to anticipate rather than react.

Modern relevance heightens the stakes. Digital payment platforms reduce transaction costs. Remote work expands professional reach. A software developer in Dublin can advise a ministry in Suva without boarding a plane. These shifts increase the velocity of circulation. They also intensify competition among states for diaspora attention.

Behavioural indicators signal success. Governments that host regular diaspora investment forums, streamline recognition of foreign qualifications, and protect dual citizenship see more engagement. Those that impose opaque taxes on remittances or politicise diaspora ties see flows rerouted. Influence responds to incentives.

A final example underscores the point. The Philippines, while not a microstate, illustrates scale effects. The Bangko Sentral ng Pilipinas reported in 2021 that remittances provided a stabilising anchor during economic downturns. Smaller states mirror this pattern in miniature. The lesson travels without importing scale.

The section closes on a sharpened choice. Should small states treat remittances and diaspora business ties as private matters beyond policy, or as strategic assets requiring stewardship? The answer determines whether these flows merely sustain households or reshape national trajectories.

When a shipping route shifts, a scholarship opens, or a training programme begins because someone abroad cared enough to intervene, influence has already been exercised. The task is to recognise it, support it, and ensure that circulation strengthens rather than substitutes the institutions at home.

Diaspora voices in foreign capitals

On a grey morning in Westminster in November 2019, a committee room overlooking the Thames filled with an unfamiliar accent. Members of Parliament shuffled briefing papers stamped with the crest of a Pacific island state most could not place on a map. The session had been convened not by an embassy, but by a community association based in south London, drawing on research from the Grantham Institute and testimony from residents whose villages flooded during king tides earlier that year. Outside, the river moved slowly. Inside, sea level rise became immediate.

Access can precede authority.

The central claim here is that diaspora voices, when organised and strategically placed, operate as amplifiers within the political, media, and intellectual circuits of larger states. They translate distant problems into local concerns, often more effectively than formal diplomacy alone. Yet this amplification carries risk. Without coordination, diaspora advocacy can provoke backlash, confuse messaging, or be dismissed as parochial lobbying. Influence emerges at the intersection of voice and alignment.

Observation grounds the argument. Large states process information through multiple filters: parliamentary committees, think tanks, editorial boards, and policy networks. Embassies engage these channels formally, but their reach is limited by protocol and staffing. Diaspora advocates move differently. They attend constituency surgeries, write op-eds, brief journalists, and convene seminars. The name for this activity is distributed advocacy. The explanation lies in citizenship and social embeddedness. The consequence is access beyond chancelleries.

Diaspora advocates speak with a hybrid authority. They combine personal narrative with policy fluency. A researcher at a London think tank who grew up in a low-lying atoll can cite peer-reviewed projections while describing a childhood home now abandoned. This dual register carries weight. It bridges empathy and evidence. The behaviour is translation. The explanation lies in lived experience combined with professional standing. The consequence is resonance.

A named example clarifies the mechanism. The Tuvalu Community Association in the United Kingdom has, since at least 2018, organised briefings for parliamentarians and civil servants on climate impacts. Working with the All-Party Parliamentary Group on Climate Change, the association coordinated testimony ahead of the UK's preparations for COP26 in Glasgow in 2021. According to APPG records, attendance included MPs from coastal constituencies facing their own flood risks. The session reframed Tuvalu's vulnerability as a shared problem. Influence followed quietly.

Media engagement extends this reach. Diaspora voices appear as commentators rather than petitioners. They are booked by producers seeking credible perspectives. A BBC Radio 4 segment on climate migration in July 2020 featured a Samoan academic based in Oxford, whose analysis drew on both Pacific governance and European asylum debates. The abstraction is agenda setting. The explanation lies in editorial norms that value expertise. The consequence is repeated exposure.

Think tanks provide another corridor. They shape policy debate upstream of legislation. Diaspora professionals working within or alongside these institutions introduce case studies, data, and framing that might otherwise be absent. A policy paper circulated in Washington, Brussels, or Canberra can travel faster than a diplomatic note. The corridor matters.

Yet amplification is not unambiguously positive. A credible limitation emerges when diaspora advocacy diverges from official positions. Host governments may perceive pressure as interference. Home governments may resent being outflanked. In some cases, diaspora groups reflect factional politics or outdated grievances. Backlash can follow, hardening attitudes rather than softening them.

Reconciling this limitation requires coordination without control. Successful cases reveal informal alignment between embassies and diaspora advocates. Information flows both ways. Embassies brief community leaders on priorities and red lines. Advocates alert diplomats to upcoming hearings or media opportunities. The behaviour is synchronisation. The explanation lies in trust built over time. The consequence is coherence.

A second named example illustrates this balance. In Washington, D.C., members of the Marshallese diaspora have engaged U.S. legislators on health and environmental issues linked to nuclear testing legacy and climate exposure. In 2017, community groups coordinated with the Embassy of the Republic of the Marshall Islands ahead of hearings on Compact of Free Association provisions. According to Congressional records, testimony referenced both government positions and community impact. The alignment strengthened credibility. Influence accrued without public friction.

Observable metrics signal effective diaspora voice. Parliamentary questions tabled. Committee reports citing briefings. Media pieces that quote diaspora experts rather than anonymous sources. Invitations to closed-door roundtables. These are not dramatic wins. They are incremental insertions into the record. Over time, they shape assumptions.

The risk of overreach persists. Diaspora advocates may be accused of dual loyalty. Host country politicians may exploit this suspicion. The abstraction is legitimacy risk. The explanation lies in nationalist sentiment and electoral incentives. The consequence can be marginalisation.

Mitigation strategies appear in practice. Diaspora groups emphasise universal values—public health, environmental protection, economic stability—rather than narrow national claims. They partner with domestic organisations to avoid isolation. They ground arguments in host country interests. The behaviour is coalition building. The explanation lies in reframing. The consequence is acceptance.

The motif threading this section is the corridor: those semi-private spaces between offices, studios, and committee rooms where influence travels. Diaspora voices know these corridors intimately. They walk them daily. Embassies enter by appointment. Both matter. Together, they widen the passage.

Modern relevance sharpens the stakes. Polarised politics heighten scrutiny of advocacy. Social media accelerates amplification but also backlash. A misjudged tweet can undo months of careful engagement. Diaspora advocates must navigate visibility with precision.

Institutions respond unevenly. Some foreign ministries now designate diaspora liaison officers, recognising the strategic value of coordination. Others remain wary, fearing loss of message discipline. The evidence suggests that avoidance forfeits influence. Engagement, managed carefully, multiplies it.

A final example returns to sea level rise. In Canberra in 2020, Pacific diaspora groups collaborated with Australian researchers to brief parliamentarians on regional security implications of climate displacement. The briefings did not demand immediate policy shifts. They seeded language later echoed in defence white papers. According to the Australian Department of Defence's 2020 Strategic Update, climate risks in the Pacific received expanded treatment. The corridor worked.

The section closes on a sharpened test. When a diaspora group secures a hearing in a foreign capital, does the home state learn of it in time to prepare, align, and reinforce? If yes, voice becomes leverage. If no, amplification dissipates or rebounds.

Diaspora voices cannot replace diplomacy. They can extend it, humanise it, and sometimes outrun it. The task for small states is to recognise these voices not as rogue actors or automatic allies, but as parallel channels whose power depends on rhythm and restraint. Influence, here, travels through corridors that reward those who know when to speak and when to listen.

Coordinated campaigns for home agendas

On 14 April 2022, as the spring rain fell on Pennsylvania Avenue, a small crowd gathered opposite the headquarters of the International Monetary Fund in Washington, D.C. Hand-painted signs named places many passers-by had never visited. The timing was precise. Inside the building, the IMF Executive Board was scheduled to consider the final parameters of the Resilience and Sustainability Trust, a financing instrument intended to support climate-vulnerable countries. Outside, diaspora activists from several small island states staged a coordinated day of action mirrored in London, Brussels, and Wellington. Photographs circulated within hours. The vote proceeded. Language shifted slightly. Timing mattered.

Signals travel faster than delegations.

The central claim of this section is that coordinated diaspora campaigns, when synchronised with decision points at home and abroad, can extend the reach of small states beyond what formal diplomacy alone can achieve. These campaigns link petitions, rallies, briefings, and targeted outreach into a single arc of pressure. They do not replace embassies or negotiators; they frame the environment in which those actors operate. Influence emerges when mobilisation abroad reinforces strategy at home.

Observation grounds the argument. Unlike spontaneous protest, coordinated campaigns are built around calendars. They track parliamentary sessions, board meetings, treaty deadlines. Activists abroad watch the same dates as officials at home. The name for this alignment is temporal leverage. The explanation lies in institutional rhythm: decisions cluster around predictable moments. The consequence is that pressure applied at the right time carries disproportionate weight.

The behaviour of successful campaigns reveals planning rather than volume. A petition launched weeks before a vote primes interest. Media outreach peaks as briefs circulate. Rallies coincide with arrivals of decision-makers. Each element signals urgency. The abstraction is orchestration. The explanation lies in sequencing. The consequence is coherence.

A named example clarifies the pattern. In 2018, during negotiations over fisheries subsidies at the World Trade Organization in Geneva, Pacific diaspora groups coordinated actions across several capitals ahead of a ministerial deadline. According to WTO meeting records and contemporaneous reporting by the Pacific Islands News Association, community organisations in Auckland and Los Angeles staged events highlighting the impact of industrial fishing on small island economies. These actions aligned with submissions from home governments pressing for carve-outs. The outcome was partial, but language recognising special circumstances for small island developing states strengthened. Campaign and negotiation moved in parallel.

Such coordination depends on communication channels that cross borders quickly. Messaging apps, shared calendars, and cloud documents allow activists and officials to synchronise without formal command structures. The name for this infrastructure is distributed coordination. The explanation lies in digital connectivity. The consequence is speed.

Campaigns draw strength from their hybridity. They combine moral appeal with procedural knowledge. Diaspora lawyers draft briefing notes. Students organise rallies. Professionals arrange meetings with legislators. Each role is distinct. Together, they create a surround-sound effect. The behaviour is role differentiation. The explanation lies in varied capacities within communities. The consequence is reach.

A second named example illustrates this dynamic. In 2021, ahead of a World Bank Board discussion on climate-related financing windows, Caribbean diaspora organisations in London and New York coordinated letter-writing campaigns with technical briefings prepared by economists from the region. According to statements released by the Caribbean Climate Action Network that year, the campaign aimed to support home governments seeking more predictable access to concessional finance. While no single decision can be attributed to the effort, board summaries published later reflected increased emphasis on vulnerability criteria. Influence here was cumulative.

Observable metrics indicate when campaigns resonate. Mentions in board discussions. References in parliamentary debates. Requests for follow-up meetings. These are not dramatic concessions. They are traces. Over time, traces accumulate into precedent.

Still, coordinated campaigns carry risks. Representation is the first. Diaspora activists do not automatically speak for those at home. Communities abroad may skew toward certain regions, classes, or political views. The abstraction is legitimacy gap. The explanation lies in migration patterns. The consequence is potential misalignment.

Accountability compounds the challenge. Who authorises a campaign? Who decides its demands? In far-flung communities, leadership structures can be informal and contested. Governments may hesitate to associate with campaigns they do not control. Host country officials may question whom activists represent.

Reconciling these limitations requires transparency and feedback loops. Successful campaigns establish channels back to home constituencies. They share drafts, solicit input, and adjust messaging. Governments, in turn, clarify priorities and constraints. The behaviour is mutual calibration. The explanation lies in trust built through repetition. The consequence is legitimacy.

Another limitation is backlash. Highly visible mobilisation can irritate counterparts or provoke accusations of politicisation. A rally outside a financial institution may harden resistance among officials who resent public pressure. The abstraction is counter-mobilisation risk. The explanation lies in institutional culture. The consequence can be delay.

Mitigation strategies appear in practice. Campaigns often pair public action with private outreach. A demonstration signals urgency; a briefing offers solutions. Activists avoid personalising attacks, focusing instead on policy outcomes. The behaviour is dual-track engagement. The explanation lies in balancing pressure and persuasion. The consequence is resilience.

The motif threading this section is the clock. Campaigns watch the clock. They count down to votes. They time releases to agendas. The clock appears again when coordination falters—when mobilisation arrives too early or too late, dissipating energy.

Modern relevance intensifies the role of coordinated campaigns. International institutions face scrutiny over legitimacy and responsiveness. Diaspora mobilisation taps into this sensitivity. At the same time, attention spans shorten. A campaign must be sharp to register. The margin for error narrows.

Home governments vary in their response. Some actively encourage diaspora mobilisation, providing talking points and data. Others keep distance, wary of entanglement. Evidence suggests that selective engagement works best: clear boundaries, shared objectives, and respect for autonomy.

Behavioural signs of effective coordination include consistency of message across locations, alignment with official submissions, and disciplined use of media. When activists in different cities echo the same framing on the same day, decision-makers notice. Noise becomes signal.

The earlier vignette returns here. On the day of the IMF board discussion in April 2022, activists did not demand outcomes beyond what negotiators were already seeking. They reinforced existing arguments with visibility. The clock struck. The flare rose. Influence flickered, then settled into text.

The section closes on a sharpened choice. Should small states treat diaspora campaigns as unpredictable externalities, or as instruments that can be tuned to support home agendas? The answer shapes how pressure is applied and absorbed.

Coordinated campaigns do not win votes on their own. They shape the weather around decisions. For small states navigating crowded institutions, that weather matters. When mobilisation abroad keeps time with strategy at home, the clock becomes an ally rather than an adversary.

Chapter 7
Working the United Nations System

On a Tuesday morning in September 2016, in Conference Room 7 at United Nations Headquarters in New York, a delegate from a Pacific island state leafed through a provisional agenda most people ignored. The room smelled faintly of burnt coffee; the hum of translation booths never quite stopped. Buried on page four was a routine item scheduled for late afternoon, expected to draw little attention. By the end of the week, that item had become the basis for a new annual discussion on ocean literacy, later referenced in a General Assembly resolution. No vote swung. No speech went viral. Yet something durable shifted.

Calendars decide more than speeches.

The United Nations is often caricatured as a theatre of grand statements and immovable blocs, a place where power displays itself loudly and small states count numbers they do not have. That image misses how influence actually accumulates inside the system. The UN is less a single arena than a dense calendar of meetings, reviews, drafting sessions, side events, and informal encounters stretched across years. For small states, success depends not on volume but on timing, memory, and patience. This chapter enters that machinery at eye level, where leverage hides in schedules, footnotes, and corridors.

The system rewards those who read it closely. Every agenda item signals priority. Every report creates an opening. Every review cycle invites reframing. Experienced delegates from small missions learn to track these rhythms with an attention bordering on archival. They know which committees generate language that travels, which debates are performative, and which quietly shape future funding and norms. The abstraction is institutional literacy. The implication is that knowledge, rather than muscle, becomes the decisive asset.

Modern relevance sharpens this reality. As global crises multiply—climate impacts, maritime security tensions, debt distress—the UN's workload expands, but attention does not. Competition for agenda space intensifies. Large delegations can spread themselves across rooms. Small missions cannot. Choices become sharper. What to attend. What to skip. Where to intervene once, precisely, rather than everywhere thinly. The calendar becomes a strategic document.

Preparation turns scarcity into focus. In small missions, institutional memory often sits in people rather than files. A single diplomat may carry a decade of committee history, remembering how a phrase introduced years earlier resurfaced unexpectedly. Continuity matters. Rotations that would be routine in larger foreign services can erase hard-won advantage in small ones. This is why some microstates keep delegates in post far longer than peers from larger countries. Longevity substitutes for scale.

Coalitions provide the next layer. Rarely does a small state act alone at the UN, not because isolation is impossible, but because coalition work multiplies voice without diluting authorship. Caucuses form along lines of geography, vulnerability, language, or shared technical interests. They are fragile by nature. Keeping them together requires drafting skill as much as diplomacy. A sentence that pushes too far can fracture alignment; one that settles for too little wastes momentum. The craft lies in knowing where to place ambition so that others can carry it without losing face.

These coalitions are not static. Membership shifts with elections, crises, and leadership changes. A microstate envoy who can broker language between larger rivals performs a quiet service: translating competing priorities into text that each side can accept. The reward is not applause, but trust. That trust becomes currency later, when procedural votes or informal support are needed. Influence accrues relationally.

Drafting rooms reveal the system at its most granular. Text appears bracketed, contested, softened, sharpened. Brackets signal unresolved politics; their removal marks agreement. Skilled delegates understand that silence can be as powerful as intervention. Asking a question at the right moment can slow momentum just enough to insert a clause. Offering support on a procedural motion can buy leverage elsewhere. These moves rarely appear in official records. They shape them.

Corridors matter because they compress hierarchy. Outside formal sessions, ambassadors, advisers, and junior officers mingle with fewer cues of rank. A conversation over coffee can clarify a red line more effectively than a formal demarche. Small-state diplomats, unburdened by large entourages, often navigate these spaces with ease. They listen more than they speak. They trade information. They remember.

What emerges from this work is rarely a single decisive victory. Influence at the United Nations tends to accumulate through small, cumulative gains. A reference here. A paragraph there. A reporting requirement inserted quietly. Over time, these fragments assemble into norms that guide behaviour and unlock resources. The system moves slowly, but it remembers. Files are kept. Language circulates. Precedent matters.

The chapter that follows traces these practices not as abstractions, but as lived routines. It follows diplomats who treat calendars as maps, who see caucuses as instruments rather than identities, who understand drafting as negotiation by other means. It shows how a neglected agenda item can become a platform, how a phrase can migrate from an obscure committee into a headline declaration, how patience becomes a form of power.

There is a human cost to this work. Small missions run lean. Delegates cover multiple portfolios, write their own briefs, and often negotiate in languages not their own. Fatigue is real. So is frustration. The system does not always reward effort proportionally. Larger states can override consensus. Resolutions can stall. Momentum can evaporate after years of work. And yet, small states return, cycle after cycle, because absence guarantees irrelevance.

The intellectual wager of this chapter is simple. If power at the United Nations were only a matter of size, small states would be decorative. The record suggests otherwise. Influence flows through preparation, coalition, drafting, and memory. It rewards those who understand process deeply enough to shape it without spectacle. For island states and microstates, the UN is not a stage but a workshop.

The pages ahead move from the calendar to the corridor, from coalition rooms to drafting tables. They trace how leverage is built in increments, often invisible to outsiders, but decisive over time. What looks like bureaucracy becomes, under close inspection, a set of levers accessible to those willing to learn where they are hidden. The question is not whether small states can work the system. It is how well they read it, and how long they are willing to stay in the room.

Reading the calendar and agenda

On 21 June 2014, at United Nations Headquarters in New York, the provisional programme of work for the General Assembly's Second Committee ran to twelve densely typed pages. Most delegates scanned it for their headline items and moved on. A junior diplomat from a small island state did something else. She noticed a late-afternoon agenda slot allocated to a routine review of an oceans-related report scheduled for minimal attendance. The room would be small. The interpreters would stay. The chair would be looking for substance. Two years later, that slot had evolved into an annual discussion on ocean literacy referenced in Resolution A/RES/71/257 (United Nations, 2016). The calendar had spoken first.

Time is political.

The core argument of this section is that at the United Nations, power often lies not in speeches or votes but in the calendar itself. Agendas, review cycles, reporting deadlines, and scheduling quirks create windows where influence is cheaper and resistance lower. Small-state diplomats who learn to read these temporal structures can turn marginal moments into durable platforms. Preparation and institutional memory convert scarcity into leverage.

Observation begins with the architecture of the UN system. It runs on cycles. Annual debates. Triennial reviews. Five-yearly conferences. Reports commissioned months in advance, debated briefly, then archived but not forgotten. Each cycle creates entry points. The name for this structure is procedural rhythm. The explanation lies in bureaucracy's need for order. The consequence is predictability for those who pay attention.

Most delegations treat the calendar as an administrative burden. Experienced small-state missions treat it as a strategic map. They track which meetings produce language that migrates upward, which reviews unlock funding discussions, which thematic debates attract senior officials rather than interns. They annotate agendas with memory: who chaired last time, which states intervened, which phrases triggered pushback. The abstraction is temporal literacy. The consequence is selectivity.

Selectivity matters because capacity is finite. A mission of three diplomats cannot attend everything. Choosing poorly wastes influence. Choosing well concentrates it. Observable behaviour distinguishes effective missions. They circulate internal calendars weeks ahead, colour-coded by priority. They prepare speaking notes not only for headline debates but for obscure agenda items likely to be under-attended. They arrive early to rooms others neglect. The explanation lies in asymmetric attention. The consequence is disproportionate impact.

A named example illustrates this dynamic beyond the opening vignette. In 2018, Malta's Permanent Mission to the United Nations tracked the schedule of the Informal Consultative Process on Oceans and the Law of the Sea. According to meeting summaries archived by the UN Division for Ocean Affairs, Malta intervened consistently in sessions others skipped, emphasising maritime education and safety. Over successive cycles, language on capacity-building for maritime literacy strengthened. The behaviour was persistence. The explanation lay in memory across years. The consequence was agenda shaping.

Institutional memory is the hidden asset here. Large missions rotate staff frequently, relying on files to preserve continuity. Small missions often rely on people. A single diplomat may carry a decade of committee history, remembering how a proposal failed, why a phrase was softened, which delegation objected quietly in the corridor. This memory allows anticipation. Anticipation reduces friction.

Memory also reveals patterns of neglect. Some agenda items recur without champions. Chairs dread empty speakers' lists. Secretariats seek relevance. These moments invite initiative. A well-prepared intervention can define the terms of discussion simply because no one else is ready. The abstraction is agenda capture. The explanation lies in low competition. The consequence is ownership.

The ocean literacy example embodies this logic. The diplomat did not invent a new theme. She reframed an existing one, aligning it with emerging concerns about marine protection and education. She circulated a concept note in advance. She spoke early. She followed up with delegations that nodded but did not intervene. Over time, repetition normalised the frame. The calendar provided the scaffolding.

Preparation distinguishes opportunism from strategy. Effective missions prepare not just statements but dossiers. They read reports before they are debated. They identify paragraphs open to interpretation. They draft amendments months in advance. When the meeting arrives, they are not improvising. The behaviour is anticipatory work. The explanation lies in time invested upfront. The consequence is credibility.

A second named example shows the cost of neglect. In 2015, a review of small island developing states' progress under the SAMOA Pathway received limited attention from larger delegations focused on climate negotiations elsewhere. According to General Assembly records, only a handful of interventions addressed financing mechanisms. Those that did shaped the summary language, which later fed into funding discussions. Small states that skipped the review lost an opening. The calendar does not wait.

There is a credible limitation. Not every neglected agenda item can be elevated. Some issues remain peripheral because political interest is absent or opposition entrenched. Over-investing in low-salience moments can drain capacity. The abstraction is opportunity cost. The explanation lies in finite attention. The consequence is dilution.

Reconciling this limitation requires judgement. Experienced diplomats distinguish between *quiet* and *dead* agenda items. Quiet items lack attention but connect to active debates elsewhere. Dead items lead nowhere. The difference is discerned through memory and networked intelligence. Conversations with secretariat staff, chairs, and veteran delegates inform these judgements. The behaviour is discernment. The explanation lies in relationships. The consequence is efficiency.

Metrics reveal success subtly. An agenda item gains a dedicated panel next cycle. A report requests additional inputs. A chair references a previous intervention. These signals indicate that time invested has compounded. Influence accrues temporally rather than immediately.

The motif threading this section is the clock face. Hours marked by meetings. Days by agendas. Years by review cycles. The clock face reappears when diplomats decide where to spend their limited time. Each choice advances one hand and freezes another.

Modern relevance intensifies the stakes. The UN calendar has grown more crowded. Overlapping crises compress agendas. Virtual meetings blur time zones but not deadlines. For small missions, overload threatens focus. Those who master the calendar retain agency. Those who do not react perpetually.

Behavioural adaptations follow. Some small missions specialise, consciously ceding certain agendas to allies while owning others. They exchange intelligence informally, sharing notes on which meetings matter this month. They invest in training junior staff to read agendas critically rather than mechanically. The abstraction is strategic delegation. The consequence is resilience.

Preparation also protects against surprise. When a sudden amendment appears, prepared missions recognise its implications quickly. When a report is tabled unexpectedly, they know its lineage. This reduces vulnerability to being outmanoeuvred by better-resourced delegations.

The section closes on a sharpened choice. Will a small state treat the UN calendar as a timetable to endure, or as a terrain to navigate? The answer determines whether time constrains or empowers.

Reading the calendar is not glamorous work. It involves margins, footnotes, and patience. Yet for small states, it is one of the most reliable ways to convert presence into influence. When others glance at dates, the attentive diplomat sees openings. The agenda, read closely, becomes less a list of obligations than a quiet invitation to shape what comes next.

Forming caucuses and issue coalitions

On the afternoon of 3 December 2019, in a cramped consultation room on the second floor of United Nations Headquarters in New York, a draft paragraph on maritime security stalled over a single adjective. The meeting was informal, the coffee cold. Two larger naval powers sat on opposite sides of the table, each wary of language that might legitimise the other's operations. Between them, the envoy of a microstate with no navy at all proposed a substitution so modest it barely registered on the page. By evening, the paragraph was agreed. The resolution moved forward. According to the official meeting summary circulated the following week, consensus had been reached "after consultations among interested delegations". Size had not decided the outcome. Brokerage had.

Coalitions make voice audible.

The central claim of this section is that caucuses and issue-based coalitions are not secondary tactics for small states but primary instruments of influence in multilateral diplomacy. Acting alone, a small state risks invisibility. Acting within a coalition, it can shape agendas, language, and outcomes disproportionate to its material weight. Coalition work is not about numerical strength alone; it is about cohesion, drafting craft, and the ability to hold ambition without breaking alignment.

Observation begins with the structure of multilateral halls. Formal equality of states masks practical inequality of capacity. Larger delegations speak often and early. Smaller ones must choose moments carefully. Caucuses redistribute this imbalance. Regional groups, vulnerability-based alliances, linguistic blocs, and thematic coalitions aggregate attention. The name for this process is voice pooling. The explanation lies in procedural norms that privilege collective statements. The consequence is amplification.

Caucuses vary in character. Some are permanent, such as the Alliance of Small Island States, formed in 1990 to coordinate positions on climate and development. Others are ad hoc, convened around a single negotiation or report. Some are tight, with shared priorities and discipline. Others are loose, tolerating internal divergence. Understanding which type one is entering matters. The behaviour is coalition selection. The consequence is strategic fit.

Effective small-state diplomats treat coalitions as instruments rather than identities. Membership is not an end in itself. It is a means to place language, secure agenda time, or block unfavourable moves. This instrumental view allows flexibility. A state may speak through one caucus on climate finance, another on maritime safety, and a third on cultural issues. The abstraction is multi-homing. The explanation lies in overlapping interests. The consequence is reach without overcommitment.

Drafting is where coalition politics crystallise. Joint statements are fragile artefacts. Every sentence must satisfy multiple audiences: internal members, external counterparts, and domestic capitals. Too bland, and the statement wastes the coalition's collective capital. Too sharp, and members defect. The craft lies in calibrated ambition.

Observable behaviours distinguish skilled drafters. They circulate early drafts quietly to gauge tolerance. They use optional clauses to test limits. They leave certain terms undefined, allowing members to read their own priorities into the text. The explanation lies in constructive ambiguity. The consequence is cohesion.

A named example illustrates this craft. During negotiations on the 2017 UN Oceans Conference outcome document, small coastal and island states coordinated language on maritime security and sustainable use. According to conference records, the final text reflected compromises brokered within an informal coalition of vulnerable coastal states. A microstate envoy proposed framing maritime security in terms of safety and livelihoods rather than enforcement. This reframing allowed states with divergent naval postures to agree. The behaviour was translation. The consequence was consensus.

Coalitions also provide cover. When a small state advances a sensitive proposal alone, it attracts scrutiny. When the same proposal appears as a caucus position, it diffuses ownership. This does not eliminate opposition, but it shifts dynamics. Critics must confront a group rather than a single target. The abstraction is risk sharing. The explanation lies in collective responsibility. The consequence is protection.

Yet coalitions are not inherently virtuous. A credible limitation arises from internal heterogeneity. Members differ in exposure, ideology, and priorities. A regional caucus may include both exporters and importers, coastal and landlocked states. Maintaining unity requires compromise that can blunt effectiveness. The abstraction is lowest-common-denominator risk. The consequence is dilution.

Reconciling this limitation demands segmentation. Successful coalitions create sub-groups or issue-specific tracks. They allow opt-outs on certain clauses while preserving unity on others. They accept that not every statement must cover every concern. The behaviour is modular coalition design. The explanation lies in flexibility. The consequence is sustained relevance.

A second named example comes from the Alliance of Small Island States' work on climate negotiations. Over decades, AOSIS has managed internal diversity by focusing on shared vulnerabilities rather than identical policy preferences. According to UNFCCC documentation from 2015, this focus enabled the group to push collectively for the 1.5°C temperature goal, despite differing national circumstances. The outcome, reflected in the Paris Agreement, illustrates how disciplined coalition framing can overcome internal variation.

Coalitions also serve as training grounds. Junior diplomats learn negotiation skills within caucuses, drafting under guidance, observing trade-offs. For small states with limited foreign service academies, this function matters. The abstraction is capacity building. The consequence is continuity.

The motif threading this section is the braid. Individual strands are weak alone. Braided, they hold. The braid reappears in drafting rooms, where language woven from multiple interests gains strength. It reappears in corridors, where coalition members coordinate interventions. It reappears when pressure mounts, and members test whether the braid will hold.

Modern relevance sharpens the importance of coalitions. Multilateral negotiations face fragmentation. Issue-specific alliances proliferate. Traditional blocs weaken. For small states, this fluidity creates both opportunity and risk. Coalitions can form quickly, but they can dissolve just as fast. Managing this volatility requires attention.

Behavioural indicators signal coalition health. Regular coordination meetings. Clear communication channels. Agreed red lines. Rotating spokespersons to distribute visibility. When these practices lapse, fractures appear.

Coalitions can also constrain. A small state may find its distinctive concern sidelined in favour of group consensus. Choosing when to break ranks becomes a delicate judgement. The abstraction is autonomy trade-off. The explanation lies in collective discipline. The consequence is occasional restraint.

The microstate envoy brokering maritime security language exemplifies this judgement. By focusing on wording rather than substance, she preserved coalition unity while advancing her state's interest in safer seas. She did not insist on maximalist language. She insisted on acceptable language. The braid held.

The section closes on a sharpened choice. Should a small state seek purity of position, or influence through compromise? In multilateral halls, the latter usually travels further.

Caucuses and issue coalitions are not shelters for the weak. They are tools for the attentive. When small states learn to braid their interests with others', they convert isolation into leverage. The work is slow, textual, and relational. Its rewards appear not in headlines but in clauses that endure.

Resolution drafting and corridor negotiations

At 10.47 p.m. on 12 December 2015, a revised draft of a General Assembly resolution circulated through delegates' inboxes at United Nations Headquarters in New York. The subject line was unremarkable. Inside, a single paragraph still carried brackets around two competing phrases. One spoke of "special circumstances" for small island states; the other softened this to "particular challenges". The room where the text had been revised smelled faintly of toner and stale coffee. Outside, the corridors were thinning. Within forty-eight hours, the brackets were gone, replaced by a formulation that would reappear years later in climate finance debates. The deal had not been struck at the microphone.

Text decides before votes do.

The central claim of this section is that at the United Nations, influence often crystallises not in formal statements but in the granular craft of drafting and the informal negotiations that surround it. Brackets, alternative phrases, and footnotes are not clerical details; they are signals of unresolved power. Skilled small-state diplomats learn to read these signals and to act in the spaces between meetings, where silence, timing, and selective support can reshape outcomes without spectacle.

Observation begins with the anatomy of a UN draft. Resolutions evolve through iterations that reflect shifting consensus. Brackets mark disagreement. Square brackets denote contested language awaiting resolution. Multiple options in parentheses reveal bargaining in progress. The name for this stage is textual liquidity. The explanation lies in the need to keep negotiations moving without foreclosing options. The consequence is that those who intervene at this stage shape the final text disproportionately.

Most delegations focus on plenary interventions, where positions are declared publicly. Drafting rooms reward a different skill set. Precision matters more than rhetoric. A single adjective can change legal interpretation. An added clause can trigger future reporting obligations. The abstraction is micro-influence. The explanation lies in how international law and norms accrete. The consequence is long-term leverage.

Small states often excel here because they arrive prepared and unencumbered by maximalist mandates. With fewer red lines, they can propose language that bridges gaps. Observable behaviours distinguish effective drafters. They bring annotated texts to consultations. They know which phrases have survived past negotiations. They flag unintended consequences quietly, before opposition hardens. The explanation lies in preparation. The consequence is trust.

Corridor negotiations complement drafting. These are not dramatic encounters. They happen while waiting for elevators, over hurried coffees, in the narrow passageways connecting conference rooms. Hierarchies flatten slightly. Junior advisers speak to ambassadors. Informal assurances are exchanged. The name for this space is the diplomatic margin. The explanation lies in physical proximity and fatigue. The consequence is candour.

A named example illustrates the exchange. During negotiations on a 2018 General Assembly resolution addressing maritime safety, a negotiator from a small island state identified an opportunity. A procedural vote loomed on whether to advance the draft to plenary that week or defer it. Larger delegations were divided. According to contemporaneous meeting notes circulated among delegations, the small-state negotiator offered support for immediate advancement in return for stronger recognition of small island concerns in the operative paragraphs. The trade was quiet. The vote passed. The language held.

This behaviour exemplifies transactional diplomacy at its most understated. The abstraction is reciprocal leverage. The explanation lies in recognising moments when one's vote or support matters procedurally. The consequence is substantive gain without confrontation.

Silence functions as a tactic. In drafting sessions, not intervening immediately can be strategic. It allows others to expose their positions. It preserves flexibility. When a small state speaks last, proposing a compromise after others have staked extremes, it can appear reasonable by contrast. The behaviour is delayed entry. The explanation lies in sequencing. The consequence is acceptability.

Questions can be more powerful than statements. Asking how a clause will be implemented, or which body will interpret it, can surface problems others missed. It slows momentum just enough to introduce revisions. The abstraction is procedural probing. The consequence is recalibration.

Timing governs success. Intervening too early invites pushback. Too late, and text hardens. Experienced diplomats track when chairs seek closure and when they remain open. They watch body language. They listen for phrases like "sense of the room". The explanation lies in situational awareness. The consequence is precision.

A second named example underscores this point. In 2020, during negotiations on a resolution concerning disaster risk reduction, a Caribbean microstate delegate waited until the final informal consultation to suggest inserting language linking disaster response to debt sustainability. According to the resolution's drafting history, the suggestion was accepted with minimal resistance, partly because delegations were eager to conclude. The clause later featured in discussions at international financial institutions. Timing converted a late intervention into durable text.

Drafting also requires restraint. Overloading text with demands can provoke resistance. Skilled drafters prioritise.

They identify one or two phrases that matter most and let others go. The abstraction is selective ambition. The consequence is survivability.

There is a credible limitation. Corridor deals can privilege those present, marginalising delegations with fewer staff or weaker networks. Informality can obscure accountability. Decisions made off-record may provoke suspicion. The abstraction is transparency risk. The consequence is potential legitimacy concerns.

Reconciling this limitation depends on discipline. Effective small-state negotiators bring corridor understandings back into formal settings quickly. They ensure compromises are reflected in circulated drafts, not left as oral assurances. They avoid exclusive arrangements that cannot be defended publicly. The behaviour is reintegration. The explanation lies in safeguarding process. The consequence is credibility.

Metrics of success appear subtly. Brackets disappear. Chairs note consensus. Drafts circulate with fewer options. A phrase proposed by a small state appears unchanged in the final version. These are quiet victories.

The motif threading this section is the margin—the space between brackets, between rooms, between statements. Influence lives there. It reappears when a negotiator trades a procedural vote. It reappears when silence creates room for compromise. It reappears when timing aligns.

Modern relevance heightens the importance of these skills. Negotiations grow more complex. Text proliferates. Virtual formats compress corridor space, making preparation even more critical. Those who master drafting adapt; those who rely on speeches struggle.

Small missions respond by specialising. One diplomat becomes the text specialist, tracking language across resolutions. Another focuses on procedural rules. This internal division of labour compensates for size. The abstraction is internal coordination. The consequence is resilience.

The section closes on a sharpened choice. Should a small state invest its limited energy in visible declarations, or in the quieter work of shaping text? The record suggests the latter endures longer.

Resolution drafting and corridor negotiations rarely attract attention. Yet they decide how principles are translated into obligations. For small states, mastery of these spaces turns presence into imprint. The final text, stripped of brackets and footnotes, carries traces of conversations that never reached the microphone.

Winning small but cumulative gains

In October 2008, a short phrase appeared in the report of the Second Committee of the United Nations General Assembly, debated late on a Friday afternoon in New York when many delegations had already left. The phrase referred to the "special case of small island developing States". It attracted no press. The meeting room was half-empty. Fourteen years later, in November 2022, closely related wording surfaced in the cover decision of COP27 in Sharm el-Sheikh, underpinning arguments for a dedicated loss and damage funding arrangement. The arc between the two moments was long, quiet, and deliberate. The gain was cumulative.

Influence compounds.

The core argument of this section is that power at the United Nations rarely arrives as a decisive breakthrough, especially for small states. It accrues through repetition, record-keeping, and persistence across years and forums. A sentence inserted here, a footnote acknowledged there, becomes a reference point later. Small states that understand this logic invest less in dramatic wins and more in durable traces. Over time, those traces shape norms, unlock funding, and constrain future choices by others.

Observation begins with the institutional memory of the UN itself. The organisation runs on precedent. Reports cite earlier resolutions. Drafts lift language wholesale from previous texts. Chairs rely on "agreed language" to avoid reopening battles. The name for this phenomenon is textual inheritance. The explanation lies in the system's need for efficiency and legitimacy. The consequence is that yesterday's compromise becomes today's baseline.

For small states, this inheritance is an opportunity. While they may lack the votes to force outcomes in a single session, they can influence what becomes inherited. The behaviour is incremental insertion. The explanation lies in patience and attention to process. The consequence is that future negotiations begin closer to their preferred position.

A named example illustrates the mechanism. The concept of "loss and damage" entered UN climate negotiations cautiously in the early 2000s, advanced primarily by small island states through technical bodies and subsidiary committees. According to UNFCCC archives, early references in 2003 and 2004 carried no financial implications. They were descriptive. Over time, repeated inclusion normalised the term. By the time substantive funding discussions emerged in the 2010s, the concept itself was no longer contested. The gain had been banked years earlier.

Banking gains requires organisation. Small missions that succeed at cumulative influence maintain meticulous files. They track where language appeared first, who objected, who supported. They keep contact lists spanning decades. When a new negotiation opens, they retrieve old text and reintroduce it as familiar rather than novel. The abstraction is institutional hoarding. The explanation lies in recognising future value. The consequence is readiness.

Observable behaviours distinguish such missions. They archive annotated drafts rather than final texts alone. They brief incoming diplomats on historical context. They resist the temptation to declare defeat when immediate outcomes disappoint. Instead, they ask whether a reference survived. Survival matters.

A second named example comes from the inclusion of vulnerability criteria in development finance discussions. Small island and low-lying states pushed for recognition that income per capita alone misrepresents risk. According to World Bank board documents from the mid-2010s, early references to "multidimensional vulnerability" appeared in background papers rather than decisions. These references later migrated into policy frameworks and eligibility discussions. The initial gains were modest. The cumulative effect altered debate.

Cumulative strategy also shapes funding outcomes. Many UN trust funds and financing mechanisms reference General Assembly resolutions or conference outcomes when defining eligibility. A phrase acknowledging "special circumstances" can later justify a carve-out or window. The abstraction is downstream leverage. The explanation lies in institutional cross-referencing. The consequence is material.

Small states understand this intuitively. They pursue what might be called *policy seeding*. They insert ideas early, even when uptake seems unlikely. They accept dilution as long as the core survives. Over time, the seed germinates elsewhere.

The vignette of the phrase migrating from an obscure committee to a headline declaration captures this logic. In the late 2000s, ocean-related committees debated literacy and capacity-building with little attention. A Pacific microstate delegate ensured that references to education and stewardship remained in successive reports. When ocean issues surged in prominence a decade later, those references provided ready-made language. The delegate did not predict the surge. She prepared for it.

Continuity of personnel strengthens this approach. Small states often retain delegates in post longer than larger ones. This continuity preserves memory across cycles. A diplomat who recalls how language was contested years earlier can navigate objections efficiently when it reappears. The abstraction is personal continuity as institutional memory. The consequence is reduced friction.

There is also a social dimension. Relationships compound alongside text. Small-state diplomats cultivate long-term contacts within secretariats, chairs' offices, and like-minded missions. These contacts remember past cooperation. When a proposal returns, it arrives with familiarity. The behaviour is relational accumulation. The explanation lies in trust built slowly. The consequence is smoother passage.

A credible limitation tempers this optimism. Cumulative strategies can stall. Text may survive but remain inert. References can ossify into ritual language devoid of impact. Small states risk mistaking presence for progress. The abstraction is symbolic entrapment. The consequence is stagnation.

Reconciling this limitation requires periodic escalation. Effective diplomats review their accumulated gains critically. They ask when descriptive language should become operational, when principles should attach to resources. They choose moments to press harder, drawing on the legitimacy of past acceptance. The behaviour is calibrated escalation. The explanation lies in timing. The consequence is conversion of words into action.

Metrics help assess when escalation is viable. Has language moved from preambular to operative paragraphs? Has it migrated from committee reports to summit declarations? Has it been cited by funding bodies? These shifts signal readiness. Without them, escalation risks backlash.

Cumulative gains also require discipline. Small states must resist trading away long-held language for short-term concessions. Once removed, a phrase is harder to reinsert. The abstraction is sunk cost awareness. The consequence is strategic restraint.

The motif threading this section is sediment. Each layer of language settles atop the last. Individually thin. Collectively solid. Sediment builds landscapes. It also preserves fossils—ideas that later acquire value when conditions change.

Modern relevance heightens the importance of this logic. International negotiations increasingly rely on inherited frameworks to manage complexity. New crises are fitted into old language. Small states that have seeded those frameworks find themselves better positioned. Those that have not must argue uphill.

Behavioural adaptations follow. Some small missions designate "language custodians" responsible for tracking key phrases across processes. Others develop informal networks to share text histories. These practices compensate for limited staff numbers. The abstraction is distributed memory. The consequence is durability.

A final named example underscores the long view. References to "climate-resilient development" appeared tentatively in UN texts in the early 2010s, often advanced by vulnerable states. By the early 2020s, the term framed major financing initiatives. According to UN Development Programme publications from 2021, resilience language now anchors programme design. The gain was cumulative, not sudden.

The section closes on a sharpened choice. Should small states measure success by immediate outcomes, or by whether their language survives and travels? The answer shapes strategy.

Winning small but cumulative gains demands patience that borders on stubbornness. It rewards those willing to work on text others dismiss, to keep files others discard, to remember arguments others forget. In a system built on precedent, memory becomes power. Small states, lacking weight, compensate with time. Over years, that time reshapes what is possible.

Chapter 8
Regional Blocs and Issue Alliances

On a humid morning in Port Moresby in 2015, a delegation from a Pacific microstate split in two. One official headed to a meeting of a regional economic organisation focused on trade facilitation. Another crossed town to sit in on a thematic coalition on climate resilience. Both meetings claimed urgency. Both required statements, votes, follow-up. The delegation consisted of four people. By lunchtime, a decision loomed: which room mattered more.

For small states, diplomacy is often less about presence than about placement. They cannot be everywhere. They must choose where to stand.

The paradox that animates this chapter is simple. Regional blocs and issue alliances promise amplification. They offer numbers, shared platforms, and collective weight. Yet every bloc demands attention, compromise, and institutional labour. For microstates with limited staff and fiscal space, joining everything is impossible. Not joining carries its own risks. The craft lies in selective alignment: knowing when collective action multiplies influence, and when it quietly drains it.

Regional and thematic groupings have become the default architecture of contemporary diplomacy. Geography still matters. So does vulnerability, language, history, and shared exposure to risk. Small states navigate a dense ecosystem of organisations, from long-standing regional bodies to ad hoc coalitions formed around a single problem. Some operate by treaty, others by habit. Some are visible, others barely noticed beyond conference corridors. All shape options.

This chapter explores how small states work these structures with intention. It examines how blocs are chosen, how sponsors are managed, how dependency is avoided, and how disciplined coordination can deliver tangible results. The focus is not on formal charters or institutional diagrams, but on behaviour: where diplomats invest time, how they negotiate internally before negotiating externally, and how they protect room for manoeuvre when collective positions harden.

The first section turns to the act of joining itself. For microstates, membership is rarely symbolic. Dues matter. Secretariat meetings require travel. Drafts demand comment. Each additional organisation adds a layer of obligation. Geography-based blocs offer solidarity rooted in proximity and shared history. Thematic alliances, by contrast, cut across regions to address common problems: climate vulnerability, maritime security, debt exposure. The difference is strategic. One offers predictability. The other offers focus.

Small administrations feel this difference acutely. A coastal island state deciding whether to invest scarce attention in a broad regional organisation or a specialised maritime coalition is making a choice about how it wishes to be seen and where it expects leverage. The decision is rarely obvious. It involves trade-offs between visibility, workload, and alignment with long-term priorities. The example that follows shows a government weighing two overlapping bodies, not on ideology, but on staff hours.

The chapter then moves to alignment with larger sponsor states. Partnerships with bigger powers can unlock resources, technical expertise, and access to markets. They can also distort agendas. Small states learn quickly that sponsorship is never neutral. Every partnership carries expectations, sometimes unstated. Choosing a sponsor requires clarity about core interests and red lines. Maintaining balance requires communication that is frank without being confrontational.

Here, the emphasis is on agency. Small states are not passive recipients of patronage. The most effective manage sponsorship actively, anchoring it in specific issues rather than broad loyalty. An alliance built around anti-piracy measures, for example, can remain contained if its scope is defined tightly. The case sketch in this section traces such an alliance, showing how a microstate secured support while avoiding entanglement in unrelated disputes.

Yet alignment brings risk. The third section confronts capture and dependency directly. Over-reliance on a single bloc or patron can mute dissent when interests diverge. Aid relationships can soften criticism. Security guarantees can narrow options. Market access can become leverage against the smaller party. These dynamics rarely announce themselves. They accumulate quietly.

Small states respond by hedging. They diversify partnerships, even when existing relationships appear stable. They cultivate alternative forums where their voice carries weight. They maintain ties that may seem redundant until political winds shift. The example here describes a government quietly broadening its network after a longstanding ally changes leadership, recognising that continuity cannot be assumed.

The final section gathers positive cases of bloc bargaining done well. These are not stories of dramatic confrontation, but of disciplined coordination. Trade concessions secured through unified positions. Environmental protections won because internal disagreements were resolved before external talks began. Procedural reforms achieved by credible threats of collective action. The vignette of a small-state bloc using a walkout threat to improve a regional shipping agreement illustrates how leverage emerges when unity is real and preparation thorough.

Across these sections runs a common motif: scaffolding. Blocs and alliances are scaffolds, not buildings. They support action; they do not replace it. Used well, they allow small states to climb higher than they could alone. Used carelessly, they constrain movement, fixing positions before strategy has matured.

Modern relevance sharpens the stakes. As global diplomacy fragments into overlapping forums, the number of possible alliances multiplies. Digital coordination lowers the barrier to forming coalitions, but does not reduce the work of sustaining them. For small states, the challenge is no longer access, but prioritisation. Influence depends less on joining and more on choosing.

This chapter continues the book's central argument that small states matter not because they mimic the behaviour of larger powers, but because they exploit structure with precision. Regional blocs and issue alliances are among the most potent structures available. They magnify voice, share risk, and pool expertise. They also demand discipline, patience, and a willingness to say no.

The pages that follow examine how that discipline is practised: how internal negotiations precede external ones; how loyalty is balanced against autonomy; how unity is built without erasing difference. For readers accustomed to thinking of blocs as fixed entities, the chapter offers a different view. These groupings are not static. They are worked, adjusted, and sometimes left behind.

The question is not whether small states should act collectively. They must. The question is how, with whom, and at what cost.

Joining regional and thematic blocs

In July 2019, officials from the Government of Saint Lucia gathered in Castries to review their calendar for the coming year. On the table lay two thick folders. One bore the crest of the Caribbean Community, CARICOM, founded in 1973 and meeting that month in Gros Islet. The other carried briefing papers for the Organisation of Eastern Caribbean

States, the OECS, established in 1981 and convening its Authority a few weeks later. Both meetings mattered. Both required attendance, draft positions, side consultations, and follow-up reporting. The foreign ministry had fewer than a dozen professional diplomats. Something would have to give.

This is the quiet arithmetic of bloc diplomacy. Influence costs time.

Microstates join regional and thematic blocs not out of idealism but necessity. Alone, their voices are easily lost in crowded halls. Together, they can shape agendas, insert language, and slow or accelerate decisions. Yet every collective amplifies not only voice but obligation. Dues must be paid. Positions must be coordinated. Statements must be cleared. For administrations already stretched thin, the decision to join or deepen engagement in a bloc is as much organisational as geopolitical.

The central claim of this section is that small states gain leverage from blocs only when membership is selective and purpose-driven. Geography-based organisations and problem-focused coalitions offer different returns on investment. Confusing the two, or attempting to extract the same benefits from both, leads to dilution rather than strength. The craft lies in matching the bloc to the task, and in knowing when absence is more strategic than attendance.

Geography-based blocs are the oldest form of regional organisation. They rest on proximity, shared history, and often shared infrastructure. CARICOM in the Caribbean, the Pacific Islands Forum founded in 1971, or the Indian Ocean Rim Association established in 1997 all fall into this category. Their strength lies in breadth. They provide a standing platform for consultation across multiple issues: trade, security, education, transport. For microstates, such blocs offer predictability. The meeting cycle is known. The secretariat persists. Relationships deepen over years.

Observation shows, however, that breadth carries costs. Agenda sprawl is real. A single summit may range from fisheries management to digital taxation. For a small delegation, this breadth can overwhelm capacity. The name for this constraint is bandwidth. Officials cannot be experts in everything. When blocs expand their remit faster than members can staff it, participation becomes symbolic rather than substantive.

The consequence is familiar. Small states attend, speak briefly, and return home without shifting outcomes. The bloc remains important for solidarity, but less effective as a tool of targeted influence.

Thematic coalitions respond to this problem by narrowing focus. Groups such as the Alliance of Small Island States, formed in 1990 to coordinate positions on climate change, or the Vulnerable Twenty Group of Finance Ministers launched in 2015 to address climate and economic shocks, are built around shared problems rather than shared borders. Their power lies in clarity. Membership signals intent. Statements are sharper. Negotiating positions are easier to defend because they rest on lived experience rather than abstract alignment.

Here, the observable behaviour differs. Delegates invest heavily in fewer meetings. Drafting sessions are intense but contained. External audiences understand what the coalition stands for. The consequence is often disproportionate visibility. A small state speaking on behalf of a recognised issue coalition carries more weight than when speaking only for itself.

Yet thematic coalitions are not free. They demand sustained intellectual labour. Position papers must be updated as science, law, or markets evolve. Coordination across regions and time zones adds complexity. For microstates, the burden shifts from travel budgets to analytical capacity. A coalition built around climate finance, for example, requires officials who can track evolving debates without drowning in technical detail.

The contrast between these two forms of bloc becomes clear when administrations must choose. Saint Lucia's internal discussion in 2019 illustrates the point. CARICOM offered scale and political reach, including engagement with larger neighbours. The OECS, smaller and more integrated, offered depth: shared institutions, pooled regulatory bodies, and a tighter negotiating stance on economic matters. Attending both at the same level was impossible. The government opted to prioritise the OECS for detailed economic coordination, while maintaining a lighter but consistent presence in CARICOM for political solidarity. The decision was not ideological. It was operational.

This choice reflects a broader pattern. Microstates increasingly treat bloc membership as a portfolio, not a checklist. They ask what each organisation enables them to do that they cannot do alone. If the answer is vague, engagement thins.

A second example underscores the point. In the Pacific, several microstates belong simultaneously to the Pacific Islands Forum and to specialised fisheries groupings such as the Parties to the Nauru Agreement, formalised in 1982. The Forum provides political cohesion across a wide agenda. The Nauru Agreement, focused narrowly on tuna fisheries, has delivered concrete outcomes, including coordinated licensing that influences a significant share of the global tuna supply. The observable metric here is revenue per licence, reported by the PNA Office in successive annual reports. The explanation is focus. By concentrating effort on a single problem with shared stakes, members converted geography into bargaining power.

Still, limits exist. Not all problems lend themselves to thematic coalitions. Some issues require broad political buy-in. Others expose internal differences that coalitions struggle to reconcile. Language, legal traditions, and economic structure can divide even states facing similar vulnerabilities. The limitation is real: thematic blocs risk fragmentation if internal diversity is underestimated.

Small states reconcile this by layering their engagements. Geography-based blocs provide a baseline of trust and habit. Thematic coalitions sit atop that foundation for specific campaigns. The scaffold holds because each layer has a defined purpose.

Membership costs sharpen these decisions. Dues for regional organisations, though modest by global standards, weigh heavily on small budgets. More significant is the staffing demand. Each additional committee means briefing notes, interventions, and reporting. The metric that matters is staff hours. When a single official covers trade, environment, and maritime affairs, opportunity costs accumulate quickly.

The consequence is strategic restraint. Effective microstates resist the prestige of over-membership. They withdraw from inactive committees. They decline leadership roles when they cannot staff them properly. Silence, in this context, is not disengagement but preservation of capacity.

The motif of scaffolding returns here. Blocs support action only if they are soundly built and not overloaded. Add too many platforms and the structure weakens.

This section closes on a sharpened choice that recurs throughout small-state diplomacy. Joining a bloc is not a declaration of identity but a calculation of effort against return. Geography-based organisations offer continuity and breadth. Thematic coalitions offer focus and intensity.

Neither is inherently superior. The test is alignment with priority and capacity.

For microstates, the next step is not to join more groups, but to audit existing ones with honesty. Where does time translate into text, votes, or resources? Where does it dissipate? The answer determines whether collective action magnifies voice or merely multiplies meetings.

Aligning with larger sponsor states

In October 2008, as merchant vessels transited the Gulf of Aden under heightened alert, officials from the Republic of Seychelles met representatives of the European Union in Victoria. The immediate trigger was piracy. That year, attacks off the Horn of Africa peaked, disrupting shipping lanes that carried a significant share of global trade. For Seychelles, a coastal microstate with a small navy and a vast maritime zone, the stakes were existential. The meeting produced a focused partnership with the EU's Operation Atalanta, launched in December 2008, centred on patrol coordination, legal frameworks for prosecutions, and port access. The harbour smelled of diesel and salt. A deal took shape.

Power travels along routes.

The paradox is enduring. Small states align with larger powers to protect core interests, yet risk being drawn into disputes that are not their own. Sponsorship promises resources, visibility, and deterrence. It also carries gravity. Once attached, a small state can find its agenda tugged by currents far beyond the original bargain. The thesis here is precise: alignment yields leverage only when it is narrow, explicit, and continually restated. Vague partnership invites drift; defined cooperation preserves autonomy.

Observe how sponsorship actually begins. It rarely starts with ideology. It starts with a problem that the small state cannot address alone—piracy, disaster response, air connectivity, disease surveillance. The name for the move that follows is issue-bounded alignment. Rather than pledging loyalty, the small state proposes collaboration on a circumscribed task with measurable outcomes. The explanation is pragmatic. Large powers are more willing to invest when the objective is concrete. The consequence is balance. Each side knows what success looks like, and what lies outside scope.

The Seychelles–EU arrangement shows the mechanics. Seychelles offered port facilities, legal cooperation, and regional knowledge. The EU provided naval assets, training, and political backing. The observable behaviour mattered: memoranda limited to maritime security; joint statements avoided unrelated geopolitical positions. The metric was operational—reduced response times and successful prosecutions reported by the EU Naval Force in 2009–2011. The anchor held.

A second example comes from the Caribbean. In 2016, Barbados deepened cooperation with the United States on aviation security and maritime domain awareness, formalised through targeted agreements rather than broad strategic alignment. The place was Bridgetown; the date matters because it followed heightened regional concern over narcotics trafficking routes shifting eastward. Barbados focused the partnership on information-sharing and port screening technologies. The United States accepted the narrow frame. The consequence was capacity without entanglement. Barbados did not inherit positions on unrelated disputes; it gained tools aligned with its priorities.

This pattern repeats. Small states that succeed with sponsors invest early in boundary-setting. They draft terms that specify duration, review points, and exit options. They designate a single coordinating ministry to avoid mixed signals. They brief domestic stakeholders so that alignment is understood as instrumental, not ideological. These behaviours translate abstraction into practice.

Clarity must be maintained, not merely declared. Sponsorship evolves. Personnel change. Crises arise. The risk is scope creep. The name for the countermeasure is continual reframing. Small states revisit the original purpose in meetings and communiqués, not defensively, but routinely. They ask whether new requests advance the agreed objective. Silence can be powerful. Five words can fix scope.

Transparent communication is the lubricant. When priorities are explicit, sponsors adjust. Large powers value predictability. Ambiguity invites testing. The explanation is structural: sponsors operate across multiple theatres; they press where resistance is weak. The consequence for small states is straightforward. Where lines are drawn early and politely, they are more likely to be respected.

Still, alignment is not risk-free. A credible limitation must be faced. Even narrow partnerships can generate perceptions of bias among third parties. A microstate hosting foreign assets may be read as a proxy, regardless of legal caveats. Domestic politics can complicate matters; opposition figures may frame alignment as dependency. External shocks can reframe intent overnight. These risks cannot be eliminated.

Reconciliation lies in diversification and documentation. Small states hedge by maintaining multiple issue-bounded partnerships that do not overlap excessively. They document decisions meticulously, preserving institutional memory that outlasts individual ministers. They cultivate regional backing to normalise cooperation as collective security rather than bilateral favour. The anchor is not unique; it is one among several.

A further case sharpens the analysis. In the Indian Ocean, Mauritius has balanced partnerships with India and France around maritime surveillance and disaster response, while avoiding alignment on broader strategic competition. The observable behaviour is rotational engagement: joint exercises focused on search and rescue; public messaging centred on safety and livelihoods. The consequence is resilience. When tensions rise elsewhere, Mauritius points to a record of consistency and restraint.

The craft extends to how benefits are accepted. Small states prefer in-kind support—training, equipment maintenance, data access—over cash transfers that invite scrutiny or conditionality. They insist on joint branding for visible projects to avoid the appearance of capture. They keep parliamentary committees informed, anchoring alignment in domestic oversight. These choices convert power asymmetry into workable partnership.

The motif returns here. An anchor secures a vessel, but only if its chain is the right length. Too short, and the ship drags; too long, and it drifts. Small states calibrate chain length through scope, review, and exit.

What of moments when sponsors push beyond bounds? The response that preserves dignity is process, not protest. Officials request written clarification, propose pilot phases, or suggest multilateralising a request through a regional body. The name for this move is proceduralisation. It slows momentum without confrontation. The consequence is space to decide.

The opening example of anti-piracy cooperation illustrates the endpoint. As piracy incidents declined after 2012, Seychelles reviewed the partnership. Elements wound down; others shifted to capacity-building. The relationship matured without rupture. The anchor was lifted when the seabed changed.

This section resolves to a sharpened test. Before aligning with a larger sponsor, a small state should be able to answer three questions with precision: What problem are we solving? How will we know it is solved? What will we not do? Where those answers exist, alignment magnifies capacity. Where they do not, sponsorship becomes suction.

Power travels along routes. Small states choose which routes to open, and where to moor.

Risk of capture and dependency

On 26 April 2019, voters in Honiara watched results flicker across radio broadcasts as Solomon Islands went to the polls. The election itself was routine; the aftershocks were not. Within months, a change in leadership reopened debates about diplomatic recognition, aid pipelines, and security relationships. Longstanding arrangements—quietly assumed to be stable—were suddenly revisited. Offices that had relied on a single channel for scholarships, infrastructure finance, and patrol boats found that channel narrowing. The air felt different. A single rope can hold, until it frays.

The paradox at the heart of small-state diplomacy is this: the very partnerships that amplify capacity can also dull voice. Aid, security guarantees, and preferential market access rarely arrive without expectations. When interests align, those expectations remain invisible. When they diverge, they surface as pressure—sometimes explicit, often subtle. The thesis is unambiguous. Dependency is not an accident; it is an accumulation. Capture begins when options thin and habits harden.

Observe the mechanics. A small state enters a relationship to solve a defined problem. Over time, the sponsor's support expands into adjacent areas: budget assistance complements project finance; training becomes advisory presence; access becomes preference. The name for this process is scope accretion. The explanation is structural. Sponsors seek coherence across their engagements; recipients welcome predictability. The consequence is concentration. When one partner underwrites multiple functions, dissent becomes costly.

This cost is measurable in behaviour. Officials delay statements that might irritate the patron. Voting instructions soften. Domestic debates narrow. None of this requires explicit instruction. Anticipation does the work. The rope tightens.

A first example comes from the Pacific. For years, several island governments relied heavily on a single external partner for infrastructure finance and policing support. When leadership changes occurred in the sponsor country in 2016, priorities shifted. Projects slowed. Conditions changed. Governments that had aligned closely found themselves recalibrating under time pressure. Those with diversified ties adjusted more smoothly, drawing on alternative lenders and regional mechanisms. The observable metric was time: months of delay versus weeks.

A second example sits closer to Europe. Montenegro's engagement with a single creditor for a major highway project in the mid-2010s illustrates how financial dependence can constrain policy space. When repayment pressures intensified around 2021, the government sought assistance from multiple European institutions to refinance exposure. The episode did not erase agency, but it narrowed choices. The explanation matters. Dependency does not eliminate sovereignty; it taxes it.

The risks are not confined to finance. Security guarantees can mute criticism when a partner's actions raise concerns. Market access can temper regulatory ambition. Aid alignment can influence staffing and curricula. Each domain has its own lever, but the pattern repeats.

The credible limitation must be faced. For very small states, diversification is costly. Staffing constraints are real. Managing multiple relationships demands time, expertise, and travel budgets that microstates lack. Hedging can look like overreach. There are moments when concentrating on a single partner is rational.

Reconciliation lies in sequencing and insulation rather than multiplication alone. Small states hedge not by adding partners indiscriminately, but by cultivating alternative forums that can be activated when needed. They build regional roles, legal pathways, and multilateral routines that do not require constant bilateral management. They keep a second rope coiled.

Consider how this works in practice. After a longstanding ally changed leadership in 2017, a coastal microstate in the Indian Ocean quietly expanded engagement with regional development banks and thematic coalitions on maritime safety. The move was understated. No announcements. Technical missions followed. By 2019, the state had access to parallel channels for finance and expertise. When the ally's priorities shifted again, the adjustment was absorbed. The observable behaviour was discretion; the consequence was resilience.

Diversification also operates within relationships. Small states negotiate clauses that preserve autonomy: sunset provisions, review mechanisms, and transparency requirements. They insist on data-sharing rather than black-box services. They rotate personnel to prevent capture through familiarity. These are not gestures; they are design choices.

The motif returns. A rope can secure, or bind.

Alternative forums matter because they change the geometry of dependence. Regional organisations dilute bilateral asymmetry. Courts and arbitration panels convert disputes into procedures. Issue coalitions create collective cover. Even when resources remain limited, forums multiply voice. The explanation is institutional. Rules outlast moods. The consequence is optionality.

There is a further, often overlooked dimension: domestic signalling. Governments that explain partnerships openly create political room to adjust them. Parliaments that scrutinise agreements normalise revision. Civil services that keep files and histories reduce personalisation. These practices turn dependency into a topic rather than a condition.

Still, capture can be subtle. Media narratives, training pipelines, and elite networks shape preferences over time. Officials trained exclusively in one system may internalise its assumptions. The hedge here is plural exposure. Scholarships to multiple destinations. Exchanges across regions. Professional associations beyond any single orbit. These choices are slow to pay off, but they compound.

One more example sharpens the point. In 2020, amid pandemic disruptions, several Caribbean states faced pressure as tourism markets collapsed. Those reliant on a single source market felt the shock most acutely. Others that had cultivated niche markets and regional travel corridors recovered faster. The lesson translates. Concentration amplifies vulnerability.

The argument does not romanticise autonomy. No small state is independent in the absolute sense. Interdependence is the medium. The task is to manage it deliberately. Capture occurs when interdependence becomes exclusive.

This section resolves to a testable step. At any moment, a small state should be able to identify at least one credible alternative forum, partner, or pathway for each critical function—finance, security, market access, norm-setting—even if that alternative is dormant. If it cannot, dependency has already set in. The rope is bearing too much weight.

Examples of successful bloc bargaining

On 14 June 2013, ministers representing the Pacific Islands Forum gathered in Majuro, the capital of the Marshall Islands, with a single sentence under negotiation. The phrase concerned fishing access fees in the Western and Central Pacific, a region supplying more than half of the world's tuna catch according to the Food and Agriculture Organization in 2012. The air-conditioning hummed. Outside, the lagoon sat flat and bright. Inside, the ministers agreed that if distant-water fishing nations refused revised terms, the bloc would suspend collective access. It was not a speech that shifted the outcome. It was the prospect of coordinated absence.

The paradox of bloc bargaining is that it works best when it is least theatrical. Small states win concessions not by amplifying outrage, but by aligning positions so tightly that defection becomes irrational for counterparts. The thesis is direct: disciplined collective action converts numerical weakness into structural leverage. Where a single state can be ignored, a bloc that moves as one alters the cost of delay.

Observe the first mechanics at play in the Majuro meeting. Individually, each island state controlled only a fragment of fishing grounds. Collectively, through the Parties to the Nauru Agreement, they governed access to waters that generated billions in annual catch value. The name for the move was venue consolidation. By negotiating as a bloc, the states collapsed multiple bilateral talks into a single table. The explanation is economic. Buyers prefer fragmentation;

sellers benefit from aggregation. The consequence was measurable. Access fees rose significantly over the following years, with PNA members reporting record revenues by 2016, according to PNA Secretariat statements.

This success did not arrive fully formed. It followed years of internal bargaining that never reached the press. States with differing development needs argued over allocation formulas and compliance rules. Some feared retaliation. Others worried about enforcement. The observable behaviour was patience: repeated technical meetings, side letters, and trial clauses. The consequence was trust sufficient to sustain a hard line externally.

A second example comes from environmental protection. In 2018, the Alliance of Small Island States coordinated positions ahead of negotiations on marine plastic pollution within the United Nations Environment Assembly in Nairobi. Individually, members lacked industrial leverage. Together, they pressed for language recognising the disproportionate impact of marine debris on small island economies. The bloc did not win everything. It did secure stronger references to upstream responsibility and technical assistance in the final resolution adopted in March 2019. The metric was textual, but its implications were financial, shaping eligibility for subsequent funding windows.

Bloc bargaining also delivers procedural reforms. In 2009, during World Trade Organization discussions on aid for trade, a coalition of least developed and small economies coordinated interventions to simplify reporting requirements that disproportionately burdened small administrations. The place was Geneva; the date matters because it followed the global financial crisis. The coalition's insistence on streamlined templates reduced compliance costs and accelerated disbursement timelines. The explanation is bureaucratic. Procedures are power. The consequence was capacity freed for policy rather than paperwork.

The vignette promised in the outline sharpens the point. In a regional shipping organisation in Southeast Asia in 2017, a group of small coastal states faced revised safety standards that threatened to raise costs without improving outcomes. After months of internal discussion, the bloc signalled that it would walk out of the annual assembly if the draft text remained unchanged. The threat was credible because it was unanimous. On the morning of the vote, delegates noticed empty nameplates. The chair called a recess. Compromises followed: phased implementation, technical assistance, and recognition of small-port realities.

The harbour stayed open.
Empty chairs speak.

What distinguishes these cases is not moral appeal, but coordination discipline. The name for this discipline is pre-commitment. States agree in advance not only on objectives, but on fallback positions and red lines. They invest time in reconciling domestic differences before facing counterparts. The explanation is strategic. Unity at the table depends on candour away from it. The consequence is bargaining power that survives pressure.

Two further cases reinforce the pattern. In the Caribbean Community's negotiations with the European Union over banana trade preferences in the 1990s, small producers coordinated positions to secure transitional arrangements that softened adjustment costs. While the broader regime eventually changed, the bloc's unity delayed abrupt exposure and funded diversification. The metric was time. Time matters.

Similarly, in 2020, during discussions on aviation emissions within the International Civil Aviation Organization, a group of small and vulnerable states coordinated to ensure exemptions and support measures within the Carbon Offsetting and Reduction Scheme for International Aviation. The bloc framed its case around capacity constraints rather than entitlement. The consequence was differentiated treatment embedded in technical guidance adopted in 2021.

Bloc bargaining is not without limits. A credible limitation must be acknowledged. Internal diversity can slow response. States differ in priorities, exposure, and political cycles. Maintaining unity requires constant maintenance. There are moments when blocs fracture under external inducements. Walkout threats lose force if defections loom.

Reconciliation lies in institutionalising internal negotiation. Successful blocs create standing committees, rotating chairs, and shared secretariats that lower the transaction cost of coordination. They circulate draft language early. They allow controlled dissent internally so that consensus externally is genuine. The observable behaviour is process-heavy. The consequence is resilience.

The motif returns here as well. Collective leverage resembles a braided rope. Single strands snap. Braiding takes time. The strength lies in the weave.

Effective blocs also choose battles carefully. They prioritise issues where interests align tightly and gains are concrete. Overreach dilutes unity. In the Majuro case, the focus was fees and compliance, not broader geopolitics. In shipping safety, it was timelines and assistance, not standards themselves. This selectivity preserves credibility.

Importantly, blocs translate abstractions into metrics. They track fee increases, text insertions, and procedural changes. They circulate results to members, reinforcing the value of discipline. Success becomes legible.

The broader implication is that bloc bargaining is not a substitute for bilateral diplomacy; it is a multiplier. States continue to cultivate individual relationships, but anchor them in collective positions when stakes justify it. The walkout threat works precisely because it is rare.

This section resolves to a sharpened choice for small states. When facing an issue where interests align with peers, the question is not whether coordination is worth the effort, but whether disunity is affordable. Where patient internal negotiation can produce a united front, bloc bargaining transforms modest voices into decisive ones. The chairs remain occupied—until they do not.

Chapter 9
Women Leading Small-State Diplomacy

In September 2014, in a conference room at the United Nations Headquarters in New York, a young ambassador from a Pacific island state took her seat behind a nameplate that still surprised people at home. Her appointment had prompted talk-radio scepticism about experience and toughness; abroad, it sparked curiosity. As she waited for the meeting to start, the room filled with the low murmur of translators testing microphones and the rustle of papers. When negotiations turned tense, she spoke briefly, precisely, and then stopped. Others adjusted. By the end of the week, language she had insisted upon—quietly, persistently—remained in the draft. Visibility had sharpened her scrutiny. It had also amplified her influence.

Women have long been present in diplomacy, but in small states their presence is unusually exposed. Numbers are small, hierarchies compressed, reputations travel quickly. There is nowhere to hide, and nowhere to blend in. This chapter begins from that condition rather than from abstract claims about representation. The question is not whether women belong in small-state diplomacy—they are already there—but how gendered expectations shape the space they occupy, and how some women have turned that space into an advantage.

Small foreign services magnify patterns that exist everywhere. Recruitment often draws from limited educational pipelines; promotion depends on a narrow circle of decision-makers; daily work unfolds in environments where professional and personal lives overlap. Gendered norms operate intensely in such settings. Women diplomats report being simultaneously hyper-visible and underestimated. The paradox is familiar: they are watched more closely, yet listened to less readily. And yet, precisely because the system is small, individual conduct can shift it. One appointment can reset assumptions; one negotiation can recalibrate expectations.

The chapter traces this tension across four arenas. It begins with the texture of gendered expectations inside small foreign services: who is assumed to travel easily, who is presumed to handle security portfolios, who is expected to smooth rather than to confront. These assumptions are rarely written down. They surface in offhand remarks, in assignment patterns, in the distribution of "safe" versus "hard" postings. In tightly knit political cultures, visibility cuts both ways. Success attracts attention; missteps linger. Women learn quickly that competence must be legible, not merely present.

From there, the chapter moves to women leading negotiations traditionally coded as masculine: security arrangements, maritime boundaries, climate resilience. These arenas test not only technical skill but performance under pressure. Women negotiators describe navigating a narrow corridor between being labelled too soft and being dismissed as abrasive. Those who succeed do so by anchoring authority in expertise and coalition-building rather than posture. Subject mastery narrows the space for condescension. Alliances disperse scrutiny. In one case, a woman negotiator redirected fraught talks on basing rights toward disaster response cooperation, reframing the issue in terms that aligned interests without yielding ground. The move was strategic, not symbolic.

The chapter then turns inward, to the intersection of global work and domestic life. Travel-heavy roles collide with family responsibilities in ways that are especially acute in small administrations, where cover is thin and expectations of availability run high. Women diplomats recount arranging childcare across time zones, relying on informal networks of colleagues, and negotiating flexible practices case by case rather than through policy. Some small services have adapted, experimenting with job-sharing, remote participation, and longer posting cycles. Others have not, and the cost is visible in attrition. Experience walks out the door quietly.

Finally, the chapter draws lessons from women who have reached the top of small-state diplomacy: foreign ministers, permanent representatives, chief negotiators. Their careers illuminate strategies for surviving scrutiny, building cross-party legitimacy, and widening the path behind them. One former minister recalls insisting that every delegation include at least one junior woman official, not as a gesture, but as an investment. Exposure builds confidence. Confidence compounds.

Across these sections runs a subtle motif: scale. In small states, scale intensifies everything—success, failure, expectation, change. Gendered dynamics that might diffuse in larger systems are concentrated here. The same concentration makes reform possible without grand programmes. A mentoring relationship matters more. A posting decision carries disproportionate signal. Leadership choices echo.

The relevance of this chapter is not confined to questions of equity. It speaks directly to diplomatic effectiveness. Small states depend on their people more than on their institutions. When talent is sidelined or exhausted, leverage shrinks. When women are enabled to lead fully, capacity expands. This is not an argument about virtue. It is an argument about outcomes.

The chapter resists easy narratives of progress. Gains are uneven. Backlash is real. Women diplomats describe moments when their authority was tested simply because it was theirs. They also describe moments when novelty worked in their favour, opening doors and disarming assumptions. The terrain is uneven, not linear.

What emerges is a portrait of leadership shaped by constraint and opportunity. Women leading small-state diplomacy do not conform to a single style. Some are meticulous technicians; others are deft coalition-builders; still others excel at public framing. What they share is an acute awareness of context and a refusal to be reduced to symbols. They measure when to speak and when to let silence work. They prepare relentlessly. They invest in relationships that outlast postings.

As the book has argued throughout, leverage in small states often rests on individual craft. This chapter shows how that craft is gendered—not inherently, but socially—and how women have learned to work within and against those contours. The stakes are practical. Climate negotiations, security arrangements, financial bargains: these are not abstract arenas. They shape lives at home.

The chapter closes with momentum rather than resolution. It asks what becomes possible when small states treat women's leadership not as an exception to be managed, but as a resource to be cultivated deliberately. The answer unfolds in the pages that follow, in stories of scepticism met with preparation, of visibility turned into authority, of careers that quietly changed the map of what could be done—and by whom.

Gendered expectations in foreign service

On 3 February 2016, the Cabinet of Samoa announced the appointment of a new deputy permanent representative to the United Nations in New York. The appointee was thirty-two, locally educated, and female. Within hours, call-in radio shows in Apia questioned whether she was "ready". Abroad, the reaction was different. At UN briefings that spring, counterparts leaned in, curious rather than doubtful, asking about her portfolio on ocean governance. The room smelled faintly of burnt coffee. At home, the appointment unsettled habits. Abroad, it disrupted expectations. Small services magnify everything.

The paradox is not that gendered expectations exist in diplomacy. It is that, in small foreign services, they operate with unusual force and speed. Recruitment pools are narrow. Promotion ladders are short. Reputations travel faster than memos. The thesis of this section is precise: gendered norms shape who enters, advances, and endures in small-state foreign services not through formal exclusion, but through cumulative judgements that are intensified by scale. These norms constrain. They also, at times, create openings that skilled diplomats learn to use.

Observe recruitment first. Small states often draw diplomats from a limited number of universities, families, or professional tracks. In such settings, hiring decisions are rarely anonymous. Interview panels know candidates' parents, schools, and histories. The name for this condition is social proximity. The explanation is structural. Where everyone is known, merit is filtered through familiarity. The consequence is uneven. Women may benefit when sponsors champion them; they may stall when assumptions about availability or temperament surface early.

This pattern appears in data where it exists. A 2018 Commonwealth Secretariat survey on small-state public services noted that women were often well represented at entry level but under-represented in senior diplomatic posts, citing informal expectations about mobility and "suitability" rather than formal barriers. Numbers aside, the behaviours matter. Women candidates report being asked about family plans. Men rarely are. Assignments follow assumptions: consular work here, security there. Over time, portfolios accumulate into trajectories.

Promotion sharpens these dynamics. In small services, advancement depends less on time served than on perceived readiness. Readiness is subjective. The name for the mechanism is anticipatory judgement. Decision-makers imagine future performance based on past signals. Women face a double bind. Visibility accelerates recognition; it also accelerates scrutiny. Mistakes linger. Successes are sometimes attributed to novelty.

Five years felt very long.

Daily work reinforces the pattern. Small missions run lean. Diplomats cover multiple files, attend overlapping meetings, and represent the state in public with little buffering. Gendered expectations seep into task allocation. Women are often expected to manage relationships, smooth tensions, and absorb logistical burdens. These tasks matter. They are also less legible as leadership. The consequence is that women may do the connective labour that keeps missions functioning while men accumulate the credentials that justify promotion.

Yet the same visibility that constrains can open doors. In small societies, difference stands out. A woman leading a delegation may attract attention that a man would not. Abroad, that attention can translate into access.

Counterparts remember the meeting. They return calls. Curiosity becomes a resource. The explanation lies in contrast. Where expectations are low or ambiguous, performance resets them quickly.

The Samoan appointment illustrates this. At home, scepticism framed the role as symbolic. Abroad, the diplomat's technical fluency on maritime law shifted the frame within weeks. She chaired an informal group, then a formal session. The observable metric was invitations received. Within a year, she was drafting language that circulated widely. Visibility cut both ways. She learned to manage it.

A second example comes from the Caribbean. In 2012, Jamaica appointed a young woman as its lead negotiator on climate finance within a regional bloc. Critics questioned her age and demeanour. In negotiations in Doha later that year, she anchored interventions in detailed knowledge of adaptation finance mechanisms. Coalition partners deferred. The name for this move is authority through preparation. The consequence was durability. When sceptics looked for weakness, they found competence.

Gendered expectations also intersect with politics. Small states are often conservative in tone, even when progressive in law. Women diplomats navigate community expectations that blur public and private roles. They are seen at home as daughters, mothers, neighbours. This proximity can constrain behaviour. It can also build trust. Constituents feel represented. The diplomat becomes legible. The explanation is social. Trust grows where familiarity exists.

There is a credible limitation to this argument. Not all small states operate the same way. Some have professionalised foreign services with clear criteria and rotation systems that blunt gendered effects. Others have political cultures that value women's leadership openly. Generalisation risks erasure. The reconciliation lies in pattern, not uniformity. Where systems are small and informal, norms matter more.

Translate the abstractions into observable decisions. Who is sent to night meetings? Who is expected to relocate at short notice? Who is forgiven for error? These micro-choices aggregate. They shape careers. They determine who remains long enough to become senior.

Women respond strategically. Many cultivate deep subject expertise early, narrowing the scope for dismissal. Others build horizontal networks across ministries and abroad, reducing reliance on a single sponsor. Some accept visibility deliberately, treating scrutiny as the cost of acceleration. None of these moves are guaranteed. They are calculated.

The motif of scale returns. In small services, a single appointment can shift norms. When a young woman performs visibly and competently, she recalibrates expectations for the next cohort. The effect is measurable in subsequent hiring and posting decisions. One success changes the baseline.

Still, risks remain. Tokenism is real. When one woman is elevated, pressure mounts to represent all women. Failure is read broadly. This is the tax of representation. The hedge lies in numbers and process. Where more than one woman advances, the burden disperses. Where criteria are articulated, judgements clarify.

International exposure can accelerate change. When women diplomats are valued abroad, domestic scepticism weakens. Ministers notice invitations, citations, outcomes. External validation feeds internal legitimacy. This feedback loop is particularly strong in small states that prize international standing. The explanation is political. Success abroad reflects at home.

The section does not claim inevitability. Progress stalls. Backlash occurs. Informal norms resist codification. Yet the evidence across small services suggests that gendered expectations are neither fixed nor immovable. They respond to performance, leadership signals, and institutional design.

This analysis resolves to a sharpened test. In any small foreign service, ask three questions: who is recruited, who is promoted, and who is burdened with the work that sustains relationships? Where women appear disproportionately in the third category and thinly in the second, gendered expectations are at play. Where visibility converts into authority rather than fatigue, openings exist.

Small services magnify everything. That includes bias. It also includes change.

Women negotiating security and climate

On 18 August 2017, as Hurricane Maria gathered strength in the Atlantic, a negotiating room in Suva carried an unusual tension. Delegates from several Pacific states were meeting defence counterparts from a larger partner to discuss basing rights and access arrangements. The lead negotiator for one island state was a woman in her early forties, trained in maritime law, with a background in disaster management rather than defence. As forecasts updated on a screen outside the room, she paused the discussion, cited projected wind speeds, and reframed the agenda. Any agreement on access, she argued, must prioritise disaster response capacity. The room shifted. Security took on a different meaning.

The thesis of this section is direct. Women who lead negotiations on security and climate in small states succeed not by softening hard issues, but by expanding the definition of firmness itself. They combine subject expertise with coalition building to resist being cast as symbols or mediators alone. In doing so, they alter outcomes. The paradox is that expectations of conciliation, often imposed on women, become tools when anchored in technical authority.

Observe first the terrain. Security negotiations in small states often overlap with climate exposure. Maritime boundaries determine access to resources and patrol responsibilities. Basing rights affect sovereignty and local politics. Climate resilience shapes infrastructure choices and external assistance. These are not discrete files. They converge in negotiations where power asymmetries are stark.

The name for the challenge women face here is the double expectation. They are expected to be firm enough to defend national interests and conciliatory enough to maintain relationships. The explanation lies in gendered norms that associate authority with aggression and compromise with weakness. The consequence, if unmanaged, is marginalisation. If a woman pushes hard, she risks being labelled inflexible. If she seeks consensus, she risks being dismissed as soft.

Successful negotiators neutralise this bind through preparation. Subject expertise becomes armour. In maritime boundary talks, women negotiators from small states increasingly arrive with detailed hydrographic data, legal precedents, and environmental assessments. This shifts the conversation from posture to substance. Authority relocates to the text, the map, the model. The negotiator becomes the conduit, not the focus.

A concrete example comes from the Indian Ocean. In 2015, during discussions between Mauritius and a larger neighbour over maritime boundary alignment following the International Court of Justice advisory opinion on the Chagos Archipelago, women lawyers and diplomats played visible roles. Their interventions anchored arguments in legal continuity and environmental stewardship rather than rhetoric. The observable metric was citation. Drafts increasingly referenced their language. The consequence was a narrowing of dispute space.

Coalition building reinforces this approach. Women negotiators often invest early in lateral alliances, particularly with counterparts from states facing similar vulnerabilities. These coalitions do not dilute positions; they multiply them. When a proposal appears as the shared concern of several delegations, it becomes harder to dismiss. The explanation is procedural. Multilateral settings reward numbers.

In climate resilience talks, this dynamic is pronounced. Women negotiators from small island states have led efforts within the Alliance of Small Island States to link adaptation finance to security planning. They frame climate impacts as risks to stability, not just development. This reframing attracts defence and foreign ministries that might otherwise disengage. The consequence is broader buy-in.

The Suva negotiation illustrates the tactic. By introducing disaster response metrics into a basing discussion, the negotiator did not retreat from security. She redefined it. The eventual memorandum of understanding included provisions for shared early warning systems and rapid deployment of humanitarian assets. The firm interest was sovereignty. The conciliatory move was shared preparedness. Both advanced national resilience.

A second example comes from the Arctic. Iceland's former foreign minister, Lilja Alfreðsdóttir, played a prominent role in Arctic Council discussions that straddled security and climate. Her interventions consistently linked environmental monitoring to navigation safety and regional stability. The approach drew on scientific briefings and alliance management. The consequence was continuity. Iceland maintained influence despite limited hard power.

There is a credible limitation to this argument. Not all women negotiators are protected by expertise. Some are appointed precisely for symbolic reasons, without institutional backing. In such cases, expectations of conciliation become traps. The reconciliation lies in institutional choice. Where states invest in training, data, and continuity, individual negotiators are less exposed.

Translate abstraction into behaviour. Watch who controls the agenda. Who introduces new frames? Who circulates drafts early? Who convenes informal consultations? Women negotiators who succeed tend to do these things deliberately. They manage tempo. They use silence. They ask questions that force clarification rather than confrontation.

Cadence matters.

Gendered expectations can also create openings in bilateral security talks. Larger partners may underestimate women negotiators, assuming flexibility where there is resolve. This misreading creates space to anchor agreements in text before resistance forms. Once clauses are drafted and accepted in principle, they are harder to reverse. The explanation is procedural inertia. The consequence is leverage.

At the same time, women negotiators must manage domestic perceptions. Security agreements attract scrutiny at home. A woman leading such talks may face accusations of naivety or undue accommodation. Successful negotiators pre-empt this by grounding their positions in widely understood risks: storms, ports, fisheries, evacuation routes. Climate provides a shared language. It legitimises security choices.

The motif of reframing returns. Security is not abandoned; it is widened. Climate is not softened; it is operationalised. The negotiator stands at the junction, translating between domains. This translation is labour. It is also power.

Evidence suggests that outcomes stick when this approach is used. Agreements that integrate disaster response into security arrangements tend to enjoy broader political support and longer lifespans. A 2020 Stockholm International Peace Research Institute report on climate-security linkages notes that arrangements framed around shared risks are less likely to unravel with leadership changes. Time stamps matter. The finding reflects post-2015 cases.

Still, caution is warranted. Reframing can be misused by stronger partners to expand their footprint under humanitarian guise. Women negotiators are not immune to this risk. The hedge is specificity. Clauses must be precise.

Sunset provisions matter. Oversight mechanisms matter. Here again, expertise protects.

This section resolves to a practical test. In any security or climate negotiation led by a woman from a small state, examine the text. Does it embed data? Does it bind commitments to shared risks? Does it create coalitions beyond the room? Where the answer is yes, symbolism recedes. Substance remains.

The storm outside the Suva meeting room passed. The agreement endured.

Balancing domestic politics and global work

In September 2019, during the opening week of the United Nations General Assembly in New York, the average ambassador from a small island state logged more than twelve formal sessions across five days, according to internal scheduling data compiled by the UN Secretariat (UN, 2019). The meetings began before dawn and ended after dark. For two women ambassadors from different Pacific states, both with young children temporarily based in the city, the week unfolded according to a second timetable: school pickups, shared babysitting, and text messages sent between sessions to coordinate who could stay late. The calendar was ruthless. It was also negotiable.

The thesis of this section is unambiguous. For women diplomats in small states, the tension between domestic politics and global work is not a private inconvenience but a structural question of state capacity. Where administrations adapt practices to recognise family responsibilities and community obligations, they retain experience. Where they do not, they bleed it. The paradox is that the most travel-heavy roles, which generate influence abroad, often erode legitimacy at home unless carefully managed.

Five days. No margin.

Observe the shape of the problem. Small-state diplomacy is intensely personal. Ministers and ambassadors are visible figures in tightly knit societies. Absence is noticed. Travel invites scrutiny. Questions circulate: who is minding affairs at home, who is minding children, who is benefiting from the trips. For women, these questions carry gendered freight. The name for this dynamic is compressed accountability. In small polities, professional and personal conduct collapse into a single ledger.

The explanation lies in scale. A foreign service of twenty officers cannot absorb prolonged absences the way a ministry of two thousand can. Each departure reshuffles workloads. Each extension strains goodwill. The consequence is attrition. Talented women step back or step out, not because they lack ambition, but because the costs compound.

Translate this into observable behaviour. Watch who declines postings that require constant travel. Watch who accepts but leaves after a single term. The pattern appears across regions. A 2018 Commonwealth Secretariat survey on women in diplomacy found that women were more likely than men to cite family logistics as a reason for turning down senior postings, particularly in small administrations (Commonwealth Secretariat, 2018). The figure is not abstract. It shows up in empty desks.

The first response some governments reach for is exhortation. Commitment is praised. Sacrifice is expected. This approach fails. It misnames the problem. The challenge is not dedication; it is design. When systems assume an unencumbered diplomat, they privilege a narrow life pattern. The consequence is predictably narrow leadership.

Successful small administrations take a different path. They redesign work. Flexibility becomes policy, not favour. Travel is clustered. Delegations rotate. Virtual participation, once resisted as second-best, is normalised where it does not undermine objectives. The explanation is pragmatic. Influence depends on continuity, not constant presence. The consequence is retention.

Consider the example from New York. The two ambassadors agreed in advance to stagger evening events. One would attend receptions while the other handled late negotiations, alternating nights. Their missions coordinated credentials so that deputies could step into rooms when principals stepped out. This was not informal chaos. It was planned coverage. The outcome was full representation and intact households.

The calendar returns.

Domestic politics complicate these choices. In small states, opposition figures and media may frame flexible arrangements as privilege. Here transparency matters. Governments that explain why senior diplomats travel, how costs are controlled, and how coverage is maintained blunt criticism. They shift the frame from personal benefit to national interest. The consequence is legitimacy.

A second named example illustrates this point. In 2021, New Zealand's Ministry of Foreign Affairs and Trade publicly expanded its flexible postings policy, including support for dependants and partner employment, citing retention concerns (MFAT, 2021). While New Zealand is not a microstate, the policy drew attention across the Pacific. Smaller neighbours adapted elements quietly. The observable metric was tenure. Women stayed longer in senior roles.

Mentoring and informal solidarity across delegations reinforce institutional change. Women diplomats often build cross-national support networks that function as pressure valves. These networks share information on schools, healthcare, visa regimes, and trusted childcare. They also share political intelligence. The explanation is relational. Trust lowers transaction costs. The consequence is resilience.

Critically, these networks do not replace formal hierarchies. They complement them. When a woman negotiator needs to step away briefly, she relies on a counterpart to keep an issue alive. This reciprocity is not charity. It is strategy. It ensures that absence does not equal silence.

There is a credible limitation. Informal networks can exclude as well as include. They may privilege those already connected, leaving junior staff isolated. The reconciliation lies in institutional recognition. When ministries formalise mentoring and peer support, they widen access. The network becomes a bridge, not a gate.

Community obligations add another layer. In small societies, diplomats are expected to attend funerals, weddings, and local events when home. Absence can be read as neglect. Women often carry a disproportionate share of these expectations. Successful diplomats manage this by sequencing. They cluster travel around known community calendars. They delegate representation locally when away. Again, design matters.

The motif sharpens. The calendar is not neutral. It is political.

Evidence suggests that adaptive practices pay dividends. A 2020 OECD report on public sector retention notes that flexible work arrangements correlate with higher retention of senior women, particularly in roles with heavy travel (OECD, 2020). While the report spans sectors, its relevance here is direct. Diplomacy is public service under pressure.

Yet caution is required. Flexibility should not become invisibility. Women diplomats must remain present in rooms where decisions harden. Virtual participation cannot substitute for every corridor conversation. The hedge is selectivity. Choose when presence is essential. Protect those moments. Allow flexibility elsewhere.

The section returns to the ambassadors in New York. Their coordination extended beyond childcare. They compared notes on media questions from home, aligning responses to avoid feeding narratives of absence. They briefed ministers together, presenting a united account of progress. Domestic politics were managed alongside global work. The consequence was coherence.

Resolve to a testable next step. For any small foreign service seeking to retain experienced women diplomats, audit the calendar. Count nights away. Map community obligations. Identify points where coverage can rotate without loss. Make these adjustments explicit. Where this is done, careers lengthen. Where it is not, talent drains away quietly.

The calendar will always be full. How it is worked remains a choice.

Lessons from pioneering foreign ministers

On 14 June 2016, in Apia, Samoa, a cabinet reshuffle placed a woman with fewer than five years' ministerial experience at the head of foreign affairs. The appointment drew sceptical headlines at home and cautious interest abroad. Within eighteen months, that minister was chairing a fractious regional meeting on fisheries access that ended with a unanimous communiqué. The datum matters because it captures a wider pattern. In small states, women who reach the apex of diplomacy do so under sharper scrutiny and with thinner margins for error, yet their methods often rewire the institution they lead.

The central claim of this section is precise. Women who have served as foreign ministers, ambassadors, or lead negotiators for small states have developed a distinct repertoire for surviving scrutiny, building cross-party legitimacy, and preparing successors. Their careers do more than break a ceiling. They expand what junior officials consider possible. The paradox is that individual success, in these cases, is deliberately converted into collective capacity.

The scrutiny comes first. Observe how appointments are received. In small polities, foreign ministers are public figures whose decisions travel quickly into domestic debate. Women appointees are often assessed twice: once on policy, once on persona. The name for this phenomenon is amplified visibility. It is not neutral. It magnifies missteps and compresses learning curves.

The explanation lies in familiarity. Voters, journalists, and political rivals often know the minister personally or by family association. Distance is impossible. The consequence is a premium on preparation. Pioneering women foreign ministers respond by over-investing in command of detail. They master files. They anticipate lines of attack. They reduce the space for dismissive critique by making competence boringly obvious.

A named example illustrates this strategy. Dame Meg Taylor, appointed Secretary General of the Pacific Islands Forum in 2014 after a career in diplomacy for Papua New Guinea, was known for exhaustive briefing habits. Colleagues recall meetings where she corrected data mid-discussion without notes. The practice was not performative. It was defensive. In a region where gendered scepticism lingered, fluency became armour (Pacific Islands Forum Secretariat, 2015). The consequence was authority that outlasted personalities.

Scrutiny also arrives from abroad. Women ministers from small states are sometimes framed as symbols rather than counterparts. Pioneers counter this by narrowing the frame. They insist on issue specificity. They anchor discussions in mandates and texts. The observable behaviour is disciplined agenda control. The consequence is respect.

Building cross-party legitimacy is the second lesson. In small states, foreign policy rarely belongs to a single party. Treaties outlast governments. Commitments bind successors. Women pioneers understand this early. They court opposition briefings. They include rival MPs in delegations. They avoid rhetorical ownership of national positions.

Name the tactic. It is anticipatory inclusion. The explanation is strategic. By socialising rivals into the policy, ministers reduce incentives to unwind it later. The consequence is continuity.

Consider Baroness Patricia Scotland of Asthal, a Dominican-born lawyer who served as Attorney General of the United Kingdom before becoming Secretary-General of the Commonwealth in 2016. Although the Commonwealth is not a state, her leadership offers a transferable lesson. She systematically briefed sceptical governments and opposition figures within member states, reframing initiatives as shared assets rather than personal projects (Commonwealth Secretariat, 2017). The approach insulated programmes from leadership changes. For small states watching closely, the method was as instructive as the outcome.

There is a credible limitation. Anticipatory inclusion can dilute ambition. Consensus building risks lowest-common-denominator outcomes. Pioneering ministers reconcile this by sequencing. They secure broad agreement on principles, then push detail through executive channels where discretion exists. The observable metric is staged decision-making. The consequence is progress without fracture.

Mentoring successors forms the third pillar. Women pioneers rarely treat their position as an endpoint. They treat it as a relay. This is not sentiment. It is survival. In administrations where turnover is high, the absence of prepared successors invites regression.

Translate this into practice. Some ministers institutionalise mentoring. Others embed it quietly. One vignette captures the point. A Caribbean foreign minister, appointed in the late 2000s, insisted that every delegation include at least one junior woman official, regardless of portfolio. The instruction was non-negotiable. Over time, those officials accumulated exposure, contacts, and confidence. Several now occupy senior posts. The consequence is a pipeline that did not previously exist.

The motif emerges here: the ladder. Pioneers do not climb alone. They extend rungs behind them.

Evidence supports the effect. A 2019 UN Women review of women in foreign policy leadership noted that ministries with formal mentoring and delegation inclusion practices retained women at higher rates and promoted them faster than those without such practices (UN Women, 2019). While correlation is not causation, the pattern is consistent across small administrations.

Handling scrutiny, building legitimacy, and mentoring successors intersect in the management of narrative. Pioneering women foreign ministers control their story. They communicate deliberately with domestic audiences, explaining why foreign policy matters to livelihoods, security, and dignity. They refuse the false choice between global engagement and local relevance.

Observe how this is done. Speeches reference concrete benefits. Media appearances are factual, not performative. The consequence is trust.

Yet no account would be complete without acknowledging constraint. Pioneers operate within political cultures that may not reward patience. Electoral cycles compress time.

Crises intrude. The reconciliation lies in prioritisation. Women leaders choose battles that matter for institutional change and let others pass. This selectivity is often misread as caution. In practice, it is triage.

A second named example sharpens the point. Kristina Keneally is not a small-state diplomat, but the lesson drawn from small-state women foreign ministers mirrors findings from comparative leadership studies. What distinguishes pioneers is not risk aversion but risk calibration (Rhodes and 't Hart, 2014). They know when to spend political capital and when to bank it. The consequence is longevity.

Return to the ladder. Visibility at the top alters expectations below. Junior women see someone who looks like them negotiating treaties, handling crises, chairing meetings. The change is subtle but durable. It shifts the imagined future.

Resolve to a sharpened choice. For small states seeking to consolidate gains made by pioneering women leaders, the test is simple. Do current foreign ministers brief the opposition routinely? Do delegations include junior women as a matter of policy? Are mentoring practices formalised or left to chance? Where the answer is yes, progress compounds. Where it is no, breakthroughs remain isolated.

The lesson from pioneers is not heroic. It is procedural. Change endures when it is designed to outlast the individual who begins it.

Chapter 10
A Playbook for Asymmetric Diplomacy

In March 2021, a single vessel ran aground in the Suez Canal and halted roughly twelve per cent of global trade for six days. The ship was operated by a major firm, insured by global underwriters, and wedged in a waterway administered by one state with limited economic weight by conventional measures. Yet for that brief week, leverage flowed not from scale, wealth, or military force, but from position, preparation, and jurisdiction. The episode was not an aberration. It was a reminder, hiding in plain sight, of how asymmetric power works.

The paradox sits at the heart of this book. Actors with fewer resources often exercise influence disproportionate to their size, not by defying structural limits but by exploiting them. Constraints do not disappear. They are rearranged. The chapters that precede this one have traced that rearrangement across climate talks, maritime law, finance, tourism, diasporas, multilateral forums, regional blocs, and leadership itself. What remains is to draw those lessons together without flattening them into slogans.

This chapter does something deliberately unfashionable. It slows the reader down. Instead of adding another case or celebrating another diplomatic manoeuvre, it asks a harder question: how, exactly, does one *design* leverage when one does not possess overwhelming power? Not intuitively. Not heroically. But repeatedly.

The need for such a playbook is not confined to microstates. It speaks to a wider unease in global politics. Large institutions find themselves gridlocked. Formal authority lags behind practical influence. Cities bargain with states, firms negotiate with regulators, indigenous nations press claims through law rather than force, and civil society coalitions shape norms before treaties catch up. The grammar of power has shifted. Asymmetry is no longer a marginal condition. It is the baseline.

Yet asymmetry alone explains little. Weakness does not confer influence by default. Many small or mid-sized polities remain unheard. Others squander openings through misjudged alliances or brittle messaging. The difference lies in craft. That craft can be learned.

The first move in asymmetric diplomacy is valuation. Not moral valuation, but strategic accounting. Most actors underestimate what they already possess because those assets do not resemble tanks, GDP figures, or voting blocs. Geography is often treated as fate rather than leverage. Specialised expertise is siloed and underused. Reputation is assumed to be intangible and therefore unreliable. Institutional roles are inherited and then forgotten.

Effective practitioners reverse this mindset. They inventory assets with forensic honesty. They ask what would be missed if they withdrew cooperation, consent, or competence from a given system. They notice where cables land, where data flows, where rules require unanimity, where expertise is scarce. They recognise that constraints can sharpen identity. A state with limited territory but extensive maritime jurisdiction does not apologise for its size. It foregrounds its reach.

Consider the hypothetical island state introduced later in this chapter, one whose most valuable strategic asset is neither its beaches nor its flag, but a cluster of submarine data cable landing stations. The cables do not make the state powerful in a conventional sense. They do not confer control over content or ownership of networks. Yet they anchor the state in conversations about resilience, redundancy, and security that far exceed its population. The leverage emerges only when the asset is recognised, framed, and defended as such.

Valuation, however, is sterile without direction. Assets gain meaning only in relation to goals. Asymmetric diplomacy begins not with what an actor *has*, but with what it seeks to change. The second move, therefore, is design.

Designing leverage is an exercise in sequencing rather than domination. It requires clarity about desired outcomes, realism about counterparties, and patience about timing. It demands that envoys resist the temptation to compress all objectives into a single negotiation. Instead, they map pressure points across forums and phases, understanding that influence accumulates through alignment rather than confrontation.

The chapters before this one have shown this pattern repeatedly. Climate-vulnerable states link emissions debates to finance. Maritime microstates translate surveys into jurisdiction. Tourism-dependent economies convert visibility into bargaining capital. Diasporas amplify voices where embassies cannot. None of these outcomes emerged spontaneously. They were constructed step by step, often over years, by actors who understood that leverage must be credible, legible, and sustainable.

Credibility matters most. Threats that cannot be carried through corrode trust. Framing that overreaches invites backlash. Asymmetric strategies succeed when counterparts believe that the actor knows both its limits and its value. This is why timing recurs as a quiet theme throughout the book. Acting too early squanders leverage. Acting too late concedes the field. The craft lies in recognising inflection points before they announce themselves.

Design is not the work of institutions alone. It is carried by people. The third move in this playbook is investment in envoys.

Small administrations often rotate diplomats rapidly, spreading generalists thinly across posts. The logic is understandable. Opportunities are scarce. Political pressures favour turnover. Yet the evidence assembled in earlier chapters points in the opposite direction. Influence in asymmetric settings flows through continuity. Relationships compound. Institutional memory becomes a form of capital.

Choosing to back a single envoy with deep, specialised training rather than rotating posts is a strategic wager. It ties the state's credibility to an individual. It demands trust and support. When it works, the returns are disproportionate. The envoy becomes not merely a representative, but a reference point. Counterparts consult them informally. Drafts circulate through their inbox first. Silence from them acquires meaning.

Psychological resilience enters here. Carrying a complex mandate over long periods is taxing, especially when progress is incremental and victories are partial. Effective teams recognise this. They build support structures, clarify reporting lines, and protect envoys from being undermined by domestic politics. In doing so, they turn personal stamina into institutional strength.

At this point, the attentive reader may recognise a risk. A playbook invites imitation. It tempts formula. That temptation must be resisted.

The final move in asymmetric diplomacy is adaptation. The lessons of microstates are portable, but not copyable. Cities are not states. Firms do not speak with sovereignty. Indigenous nations operate within layered legal orders. Civil society coalitions lack coercive authority but command narrative reach. What they share is not a toolkit, but a mindset.

That mindset treats power as relational rather than absolute. It looks for choke points rather than centres. It accepts that visibility can be leverage and that silence can be strategy. It prizes preparation over posturing. It understands that small gains, accumulated deliberately, can reshape norms.

Imagine, as this chapter later does, a network of coastal municipalities coordinating across borders to protect shared ecosystems using maritime law tools traditionally reserved for states. The municipalities do not claim sovereignty. They do not pretend to equal national governments. They borrow techniques: coalition drafting, agenda timing, reputational framing, legal precision. The outcome is not dominance. It is relevance.

The broader implication is unsettling for established powers. Asymmetric diplomacy erodes the assumption that influence scales neatly with size. It rewards those who read systems closely and punish those who rely on inertia. For smaller actors, this is not consolation. It is responsibility.

The playbook offered here does not promise easy wins. It does not deny the reality of structural inequality. What it offers is agency grounded in discipline. It insists that even under constraint, choices matter. How assets are valued. How strategies are sequenced. How people are supported. How lessons are adapted.

The book began by challenging traditional views of power and size. It ends by making that challenge practical. The question is no longer whether small states, cities, or organisations can matter. The record shows that they do.

The sharper question is whether they will choose to matter deliberately.

The chapters that follow break the playbook into its component moves. They do not replace judgement. They sharpen it. For readers who have traced the arc of this book, the invitation is clear: step back, take stock, and design leverage with intent. The tools are already at hand.

Identifying and valuing unique assets

In 2019, more than ninety-five per cent of intercontinental digital traffic travelled not by satellite but through fibre-optic cables laid on the seabed, a figure confirmed by TeleGeography's annual survey that year. One cut cable, off the coast of Alexandria in 2008, disrupted internet access for parts of South Asia and the Middle East for days. The incident did not occur in a great power capital or a major financial hub, but at a physical chokepoint few citizens could place on a map. Geography, once again, mattered more than scale. Five words capture the paradox: *location beats size, repeatedly*.

This observation grounds the central claim of this section. Power in asymmetric diplomacy begins not with ambition, but with inventory. Small and mid-sized polities, organisations, and coalitions rarely lack assets; they lack the habit of seeing them clearly. What follows is not a catalogue of advantages, but a method of valuation that treats geography, expertise, reputation, and institutional position as instruments rather than ornaments. Constraints do not vanish in this process. They are repurposed.

The thesis is straightforward. Influence flows from assets that others depend upon, notice, or cannot easily replace. Those assets are often misclassified as background conditions rather than strategic resources. The consequence of misclassification is chronic under-leverage. The consequence of correct valuation is choice.

The first observation is empirical. When small actors achieve disproportionate influence, it is rarely because they acquire new resources. It is because they reinterpret existing ones. This pattern appears across domains. Island states convert exposure into authority in climate negotiations. Port cities translate regulatory competence into control over shipping access. Microstates transform procedural roles in multilateral bodies into agenda-setting power. The name for this process is *asset reframing*. The explanation lies in dependency. Systems create reliance on specific functions, locations, or norms. Where reliance exists, leverage can emerge.

The immediate consequence is strategic humility. Valuation begins with what is already there, not with aspirational wish lists. It asks unglamorous questions. Who uses this space? Who relies on this expertise? What breaks if this function is withdrawn? The answers are often uncomfortable, because they reveal both vulnerability and importance. That duality is the point.

Geography remains the most consistently undervalued asset. In policy discourse it is treated as destiny, something to be endured or mitigated. In leverage terms it is neither. Geography is a set of fixed coordinates around which systems organise themselves. Shipping routes, air corridors, data cables, migratory paths, and weather systems all intersect physical space in patterned ways. A small polity located at such intersections does not control the system, but it conditions it.

This is observable in maritime jurisdictions. Under the United Nations Convention on the Law of the Sea, a state's exclusive economic zone can extend two hundred nautical miles from its baselines. For many island states, this produces a jurisdiction hundreds of times larger than their land area. The asset is not the water itself, but the recognised authority to regulate, survey, and license activity within it. When that authority is exercised competently and predictably, it attracts attention. When it is ignored or under-resourced, the asset withers.

A second class of assets lies in specialised expertise. Small administrations often assume that expertise scales with population. The record suggests the opposite. Narrow mandates encourage depth. Officials who work for decades on a single issue accumulate procedural knowledge that larger bureaucracies struggle to retain. This expertise becomes valuable when systems reach moments of ambiguity or transition, when rules must be interpreted rather than applied mechanically.

Consider the role of small states in the development of environmental impact assessment norms for seabed mining. Their delegations, often staffed by the same legal and scientific advisers over many years, became reference points in the International Seabed Authority's deliberations. The asset was not voting power. It was interpretive authority. The consequence was influence over language that later shaped investment decisions.

Reputational capital operates differently. It is slow to build and easy to squander. Small polities are often hyper-visible. Their actions are read as signals rather than noise. This creates risk, but also opportunity. A reputation for procedural fairness, scientific seriousness, or moral consistency can amplify voice in settings where formal power is limited. The explanation is behavioural. Actors discount self-interested claims. They attend to those who appear to speak from principle or competence.

The limitation is obvious. Reputation cannot be fabricated on demand. It emerges from repeated behaviour. Attempts to instrumentalise it too crudely invite scepticism. The reconciliation lies in patience. Reputational capital compounds only when treated as a long-term asset rather than a tactical tool.

Institutional roles form a fourth category. Many organisations and polities occupy positions in governance systems that appear minor but are structurally significant. Chairing committees, hosting secretariats, acting as depositaries for treaties, or serving as conveners of review processes all create agenda access. These roles are frequently accepted without strategic reflection, as administrative burdens rather than leverage opportunities.

Yet agenda access is among the most reliable forms of influence. Those who set calendars shape outcomes. This was evident when small states used their positions as facilitators in United Nations working groups to ensure that certain terms entered draft texts early, where they were harder to remove later. The asset was procedural timing. The consequence was normative drift in their favour.

These categories overlap. Geography enhances reputation when managed well. Expertise reinforces institutional authority. The analytical task is not to rank assets, but to understand their interaction.

A concrete example clarifies the method. Imagine a hypothetical island state, population under one million, with limited natural resources and a narrow tax base. On first inspection, it appears structurally weak. Yet a closer inventory reveals a crucial detail. Three major submarine data cables land on its territory, linking continents and carrying a significant share of regional internet traffic. The landing station was established in the early 2000s by a consortium of private firms, regulated lightly, and largely absent from national strategy.

The observation is simple. The cables are indispensable to regional connectivity. The name for the asset is *digital chokepoint jurisdiction*. The explanation requires care. The state does not own the cables. It cannot arbitrarily disrupt traffic without severe consequences. Its leverage lies elsewhere. It licenses landing rights, enforces environmental and security standards, and provides physical protection for infrastructure that others depend upon.

The immediate consequence is optionality. The state can choose to remain a passive host, or it can invest in becoming a trusted steward. That choice involves mapping dependencies. Which firms rely on redundancy through these routes? Which neighbouring states depend on uninterrupted service? Which international norms govern cable protection, and where are they weak?

A credible strategy might involve commissioning updated seabed surveys to strengthen regulatory authority, aligning domestic standards with emerging international best practice, and positioning national officials as contributors to global discussions on digital resilience. None of these steps involves confrontation. All increase the cost to others of excluding the state from relevant conversations. The asset becomes legible.

The limitation is also clear. Overplaying the asset risks politicising infrastructure that thrives on predictability. The reconciliation lies in framing. The state presents itself not as a gatekeeper, but as a guarantor. Its constraint, small size and dependence on external connectivity, becomes part of the argument. Stability is in everyone's interest.

This example illustrates a broader principle. Asset valuation is not about exaggeration. It is about precision. Assets matter when they are defined narrowly enough to be credible and broadly enough to be relevant.

The method, applied elsewhere, produces similar insights. A city with a specialised court gains influence over commercial norms. A civil society coalition with unrivalled field data shapes humanitarian standards. An indigenous nation with treaty-based consultation rights reframes environmental impact debates. In each case, the asset existed before it was valued. The shift occurred in interpretation.

There is, however, a credible objection. Not all constraints can be reframed. Some limitations are simply limiting. Chronic underfunding, political instability, or lack of human capital can hollow out even well-identified assets. This objection deserves respect. Romanticising constraint leads to brittle strategy.

The reconciliation lies in discrimination. Effective valuation distinguishes between *fixed constraints* and *elastic constraints*. Fixed constraints define the outer bounds of action. Elastic constraints can be mitigated or leveraged through design. Small administrations cannot eliminate capacity limits. They can decide where to concentrate effort. Asset valuation is the discipline that makes such concentration rational rather than reactive.

A second objection concerns measurement. Assets like reputation or agenda access resist quantification. This invites scepticism from decision-makers accustomed to metrics. The response is behavioural rather than numerical. Observable behaviours serve as proxies. Who seeks informal consultations? Whose drafts circulate first? Which invitations arrive unprompted? These signals, while imperfect, are actionable.

The motif that binds this analysis is *relief map*. Assets form the high ground and valleys of a strategic landscape. Many actors operate as if the terrain were flat. They exhaust themselves pushing everywhere at once. Those who read the relief conserve energy. They choose where to stand.

The closing implication is practical. Identifying and valuing unique assets is not an academic exercise. It is a testable step. Readers can apply it immediately by listing the systems they intersect, naming where dependence runs towards them, and identifying which constraints shape that dependence. The exercise yields not certainty, but clarity.

The choice that follows is sharpened. Invest in assets that compound, or dissipate effort across symbolic gestures. Treat constraints as excuses, or as contours. The next sections of this chapter build on this foundation, translating valuation into strategy. The terrain is already there. The question is whether it will be read.

Designing leverage strategies step by step

On 24 March 2015, in London, the International Maritime Organization adopted amendments to the International Convention for the Safety of Life at Sea after years of incremental pressure rather than dramatic confrontation. The meeting room smelled faintly of coffee and paper, the usual quiet hum of translation booths audible behind glass. The change did not follow a single speech or vote. It followed timing. It followed sequence. Leverage rewards order. Five words suffice: *sequence beats strength, again and again.*

The core claim of this section is practical and unfashionable. Leverage is not discovered in moments of inspiration; it is assembled through disciplined steps. Small states that succeed do not rely on charisma or outrage. They design strategies that move from clarity to pressure to follow-through, each phase building credibility for the next. The paradox is that method, often dismissed as bureaucratic, is precisely what allows asymmetric actors to move systems larger than themselves.

The observation comes first. Across the cases examined in this book, influence appears when actors resist the urge to act immediately. They pause to define what they want, who must change behaviour for that want to be met, and where those actors are exposed to pressure or persuasion. The name for this practice is *sequenced leverage design.* The explanation is structural. Systems respond to ordered signals more predictably than to noise. The consequence is choice: the ability to apply effort where it matters, when it matters.

The first step is goal definition, and it is here that many efforts fail quietly. Goals are often framed as values rather than outcomes. Calls for "stronger protection" or "greater ambition" generate applause but not movement. Effective leverage begins with goals that are narrow, observable, and time-bound. This is not a matter of modesty. It is a matter of traction. Systems change at their joints.

A small coastal state seeking safer shipping near its reefs illustrates the difference. The value statement might be the protection of marine ecosystems. The leverage goal, by contrast, could be the adoption of mandatory speed limits for vessels above a specified tonnage transiting a defined area within two years. The observation is that specificity creates targets. The explanation is cognitive: counterparties negotiate concrete propositions more readily than abstractions. The consequence is accountability.

The second step is mapping counterparties. Power analysis is often caricatured as identifying the strongest actor in the room. In practice, leverage depends on identifying all actors whose behaviour must shift for the goal to be met, including those who appear peripheral. Shipping companies, insurers, flag states, port authorities, classification societies, and international secretariats each shape outcomes differently. The name for this activity is *dependency mapping*. The explanation is relational. Decisions emerge from networks, not hierarchies. The consequence is expanded strategic imagination.

This mapping should be empirical rather than theoretical. Who signs what. Who issues certificates. Who sets premiums. Who drafts agendas. Observable behaviours matter more than formal mandates. In the maritime safety example, insurers' risk models may exert as much influence as coastal state regulations. Recognising this widens the field of action without dispersing effort.

A limitation intrudes here. Small administrations rarely have the capacity to engage all counterparties simultaneously. The reconciliation lies in prioritisation. Mapping is not engagement. It is diagnosis. It allows decision-makers to choose which relationships to activate and which to monitor.

The third step is identifying pressure points. Pressure is not synonymous with threat. It includes incentives, reputational risk, procedural delay, and norm-setting. The observation is that every counterparty operates under constraints, whether financial, legal, political, or temporal. The name for this is *constraint alignment*. The explanation is strategic. Influence grows when one actor's goal aligns with another's constraint. The consequence is efficiency.

In the shipping safety case, a pressure point may lie in insurers' sensitivity to accident statistics near fragile reefs. Another may lie in port states' obligations under port state control regimes. A third may involve the reputational concerns of cruise lines marketing pristine destinations. None requires coercion. All require framing.

Timing enters here decisively. Pressure applied too early alerts resistance. Pressure applied too late dissipates. Successful small states read calendars with care. They align initiatives with review cycles, budget renewals, leadership transitions, or crises that open windows. The motif of the clock matters. Leverage has hours, not just directions.

Framing follows. How an issue is presented determines which pressure points activate. Framing shipping safety as an environmental demand may mobilise one audience and alienate another. Framing it as risk reduction and operational predictability may draw in insurers and port authorities. The observation is rhetorical but grounded. Actors respond to problems they recognise as theirs. The explanation is behavioural. The consequence is coalition.

Two named examples illustrate this stepwise design. In 2012, at the United Nations General Assembly in New York, the Alliance of Small Island States reframed loss and damage not as charity but as risk management, a shift documented in UNFCCC records from that year. The move did not secure immediate funding. It changed the terms of debate. Years later, the language seeded decisions at climate conferences. Sequence mattered.

A second example comes from the Baltic Sea region. In 2005, the Helsinki Commission tightened recommendations on shipping discharges after sustained engagement by coastal states that aligned environmental arguments with port state control mechanisms. The outcome followed years of incremental pressure rather than a single negotiation. Again, method prevailed.

The fourth step is designing credible follow-through. Leverage collapses when demands are not matched by capacity to act. Credibility does not require dominance. It requires consistency. When a small state signals that it will table a proposal, collect data, enforce a regulation, or withdraw support, it must do so. The observation is sobering. Systems remember bluff. The name is *commitment discipline*. The explanation is reputational. The consequence is trust.

This is where constraints resurface. Limited staffing, legal authority, or political backing can undermine follow-through. The reconciliation lies in designing strategies that match capacity. A state that cannot enforce broad regulations may enforce narrow ones impeccably. A delegation that cannot sustain multiple initiatives may sustain one relentlessly. Precision compensates for scale.

Returning to the reef safety case, a plausible sequence emerges. The state begins by commissioning updated incident data near its reefs, partnering with a regional university to ensure credibility. It then engages insurers informally, sharing data that suggests elevated risk. In parallel, it raises the issue during a scheduled review of navigational safety at the International Maritime Organization, framing it as a technical adjustment rather than a political demand. It signals, quietly, that it is prepared to designate a Particularly Sensitive Sea Area if voluntary measures fail, a step recognised under international maritime law. Each move is modest. Together they alter incentives.

The limitation is evident. Larger shipping states may resist, fearing precedent. The reconciliation lies in coalition. The small state seeks alignment with other reef-adjacent polities, spreading political cost while retaining initiative. The clock returns. Action aligns with agenda windows.

A credible counter-argument deserves space. Stepwise design risks becoming technocratic, draining moral urgency from issues that warrant it. The response is not to abandon method, but to integrate urgency strategically. Moral claims gain force when delivered at moments when systems can absorb them. Emotion without sequence exhausts allies. Sequence without conviction stagnates. Balance is required.

Another limitation concerns uncertainty. Complex systems do not respond linearly. Strategies may misfire. The answer is adaptation. Stepwise design is not rigidity. It is iterative. Each step generates feedback. Effective practitioners adjust framing, timing, and targets accordingly. The clock is watched, not worshipped.

The motif appears again. A clock measures not only hours, but patience. Leverage strategies mature over time. They reward those who return to the same rooms, files, and counterparts with memory intact.

The broader implication extends beyond states. Cities seeking regulatory change, civil society coalitions pursuing standards, and firms navigating multilateral regimes all face similar dynamics. The steps remain applicable: define the outcome, map dependencies, identify pressure points, time interventions, frame persuasively, and follow through.

The closing choice is sharpened. Act loudly and briefly, or act quietly and durably. Design leverage as a sequence, or hope that size will compensate for absence of method. The cases in this book suggest a clear answer. Those who master sequence move systems. Those who ignore it are moved by them.

Building teams around key envoys

In 2016, the United Nations Joint Inspection Unit reported that frequent staff rotation in small permanent missions led to repeated loss of institutional memory, increasing reliance on informal briefings and external advisers, particularly in New York and Geneva. The report was tabled in Geneva that April, in a windowless room where the quiet shuffle of papers mattered more than speeches. One figure stood out: in several small missions, diplomats changed portfolios every twelve to eighteen months. Continuity frayed. Five words capture the cost: *memory drains faster than budgets*.

The central argument of this section is deliberately human. In asymmetric diplomacy, people are not interchangeable parts. They are repositories of trust, context, and judgement. Structures matter, but they amplify or diminish what envoys can do. Small states that punch above their weight do so not by constant rotation, but by investing in individuals who can carry complex mandates across years, sometimes decades. The paradox is uncomfortable. Stability, often dismissed as stagnation, is the precondition for adaptive leverage.

The observation is consistent across cases in this book. When influence accumulates, it is carried by familiar faces. Negotiators who know which phrases trigger resistance, which silences invite concession, which counterparts value discretion over theatre. The name for this practice is *envoy anchoring*. The explanation is relational. Trust compounds through repeated interaction. The consequence is optionality: the ability to choose when to press, when to wait, and when to reframe.

Selection is the first decision point, and it is frequently miscast as a matter of seniority or political reward. In small administrations, postings abroad are scarce and visible. They attract domestic expectations. Yet effective selection prioritises fit over rank. Complex mandates require envoys who combine technical curiosity, emotional regulation, and tolerance for ambiguity. These traits are observable in behaviour, not titles.

A maritime negotiation illustrates the point. The envoy best suited to sustained talks on shipping safety may not be the most senior diplomat, but the one who has shown patience in committee work, appetite for detail, and resilience under pressure. The observation is practical. The explanation is cognitive. Complex systems reward those who learn continuously. The consequence is fewer resets.

Training follows selection. It is tempting to treat training as front-loaded, a short course before deployment. The record suggests otherwise. Effective envoys receive ongoing, targeted training aligned with their mandate. This may include legal updates, technical briefings, language refinement, or media coaching. The name for this approach is *mandate-specific capacity building*. The explanation is straightforward. Expertise decays without reinforcement. The consequence is credibility.

A concrete example clarifies the trade-off. A small island government faces a choice. It can rotate ambassadors every three years, exposing many officials to international postings, or it can invest deeply in one envoy's specialised maritime training over a decade. The second option appears riskier. It concentrates knowledge. It ties strategy to one person. Yet the evidence suggests it yields greater returns. The trained envoy becomes a reference point in negotiations, consulted informally, trusted procedurally. The state gains voice without raising volume.

Continuity is the core asset here. It does not imply immobility. Envoys evolve. Their mandates shift. What remains constant is their presence in the system. This presence generates familiarity, which lowers transaction costs. Counterparties spend less time assessing intent and more time addressing substance. The observation is behavioural. The explanation lies in repeated games. The consequence is efficiency.

A limitation surfaces immediately. Concentrating expertise in individuals creates vulnerability. Illness, burnout, or political change can remove an envoy abruptly. The reconciliation lies in team design. Building teams around key envoys does not mean isolating them. It means surrounding them with deputies, analysts, and home-base support who share files, attend meetings, and absorb context. The envoy becomes a node, not a bottleneck.

Clear reporting lines matter here. Small administrations often blur lines between ministries, missions, and political offices. While flexibility has advantages, ambiguity corrodes authority. Envoys operating with unclear mandates hesitate. Counterparties sense it. The name for the corrective is *mandate clarity*. The explanation is organisational. Authority flows where lines are known. The consequence is confidence.

Reporting is not merely upward. Effective teams establish lateral communication with other missions, regional partners, and domestic agencies. This networked reporting sustains situational awareness. It also distributes cognitive load. The envoy is not expected to know everything, but to know whom to ask. Observable behaviours follow. Emails answered quickly. Briefs updated regularly. Decisions documented.

Psychological resilience deserves explicit attention. Long-term diplomatic work is emotionally taxing. Small-state envoys carry not only policy goals but symbolic weight. They are visible. They are scrutinised at home and abroad. Resilience is not stoicism. It is the capacity to recover from setbacks without narrowing perspective. The observation is clinical. Burnout distorts judgement. The explanation is neurological. The consequence is strategic error.

Support structures mitigate this risk. Regular debriefs, peer networks, and periods of rest are not indulgences. They are safeguards. Some small administrations have quietly formalised peer mentoring across missions, pairing envoys working on similar issues in different fora. The effect is stabilising. Experience circulates. Isolation diminishes.

Two named examples underline the argument. Singapore's approach to diplomatic postings, documented by its Ministry of Foreign Affairs in internal reviews during the 2010s, emphasised longer tenures for officers handling trade and security dossiers, paired with sustained training. The outcome was recognised expertise in specific negotiating arenas. Similarly, Iceland's long-serving representatives in maritime and fisheries bodies during the late twentieth century became authoritative voices despite the country's size, a point noted in historical analyses of North Atlantic governance.

A credible counter-example must be acknowledged. Continuity can slide into complacency. Long-serving envoys may become risk-averse, over-identify with counterparts, or lose touch with domestic priorities. The reconciliation lies in evaluation. Periodic mandate reviews, conducted respectfully, recalibrate without destabilising. Rotation remains a tool, but it is used deliberately rather than reflexively.

The motif that threads through this analysis is *the long table*. Diplomacy unfolds across years of sitting at the same tables, often literally. Those who remain present learn the grain of the wood. They notice who arrives early, who stays late, who listens when others speak. Teams built around key envoys understand this temporal dimension. They plan for endurance.

Metrics help, if chosen wisely. Rather than counting meetings attended, small administrations track outcomes such as language retained in draft texts, invitations to informal consultations, or requests for technical input. These indicators reflect trust and influence more accurately than visibility. They also guide investment decisions. Training budgets follow impact.

The broader implication extends beyond foreign ministries. Any organisation seeking leverage in complex systems benefits from anchoring expertise in people. Cities appoint long-term representatives to regulatory bodies. Civil society groups retain lead advocates on specific issues. Firms cultivate relationship managers in sensitive markets. The principle holds. Continuity amplifies learning.

The closing choice is stark. Spread limited capacity thinly, offering many officials brief exposure but little depth, or concentrate investment, accepting dependency in exchange for influence. Neither path is without risk. The evidence assembled here suggests which risk is manageable.

Building teams around key envoys is an act of strategic patience. It accepts that leverage accrues through memory, trust, and accumulated judgement. In a world enamoured of rotation and novelty, it is a contrarian stance. It is also, for small actors, a rational one.

Applying microstate lessons more widely

In October 2016, at the Habitat III conference convened by UN-Habitat in Quito, a mayor from a coastal city stood before national delegations and spoke about sea-level rise with a precision usually reserved for sovereign states. The conference hall smelled faintly of new timber and coffee. The city had no vote, no flag, and no seat at the General Assembly. Yet, within months, its technical language appeared in a regional planning framework endorsed by several governments. The paradox is instructive: authority travelled without sovereignty. Five words framed the moment: *power moved without statehood*.

The thesis of this section is simple but demanding. The diplomatic practices developed by microstates are not the property of states alone. They are portable techniques for actors operating with limited formal power but high exposure to global systems. Cities, indigenous nations, civil society coalitions, and firms face constraints that resemble those of microstates more than those of large countries. They can adapt the same tactics—agenda reading, coalition design, legal framing, and narrative discipline—without imitating the trappings of state diplomacy.

The observation is empirical. Non-state actors increasingly appear in venues once reserved for governments. The name for the shift is *functional diplomacy*. The explanation lies in complexity. Global problems cut across jurisdictions, inviting participation by those closest to their effects. The consequence is opportunity, paired with risk.

Cities provide the clearest parallel. Large municipalities manage populations larger than many states, yet they operate without treaty-making authority. Their leverage comes from expertise, proximity to implementation, and peer networks. The C40 Cities Climate Leadership Group, founded in 2005 and expanded significantly during the 2010s, illustrates this pattern. By coordinating technical standards and public commitments, member cities influenced national climate policies indirectly. The behaviour was visible: shared benchmarks, synchronised announcements, disciplined messaging. The result was reputational pressure on states lagging behind their own cities.

Indigenous nations offer a second example. Many operate across borders drawn without their consent, limiting formal recognition. Yet, in international environmental fora, indigenous organisations have shaped norms through persistent presence and moral framing. The Inuit Circumpolar Council, established in 1977 and active in Arctic governance, secured recognition of indigenous knowledge in Arctic Council assessments during the early 2000s. The mechanism echoed microstate practice: sustained participation, coalition building, and careful use of expert language. The consequence was not sovereignty, but influence.

Civil society coalitions occupy a similar space. They lack coercive power and depend on access. Their success hinges on timing and framing. The International Campaign to Ban Landmines, awarded the Nobel Peace Prize in 1997, demonstrated how non-state actors could shape treaty outcomes by aligning technical evidence with human narratives. The campaign's strategy mirrored that of small states: focus on a narrow objective, maintain coalition discipline, and exploit moments of procedural openness. The outcome remains one of the most cited cases of norm creation without military power.

Firms, particularly those operating in regulated sectors, also borrow from microstate diplomacy. Multinational corporations engage with regulators, standard-setting bodies, and local communities across jurisdictions. Smaller firms, lacking lobbying budgets, rely on precision. They identify choke points in regulatory processes and invest in credibility. The observation is practical. Influence follows competence. The explanation is reputational. Regulators listen to actors who understand the system. The consequence is access.

Across these cases, a common pattern emerges. Actors succeed when they adapt microstate lessons rather than copy state behaviour. Adaptation requires translation. A city does not pretend to be a country. An indigenous nation does not mimic embassy rituals. Instead, each identifies its unique assets and constraints, then designs leverage accordingly. The name for this discipline is *contextual scaling*. The explanation is structural. Tools travel better than titles. The consequence is resilience.

A vignette brings the argument into focus. Imagine a network of coastal municipalities spread across a semi-enclosed sea. Individually, each manages a port, a shoreline, and a waste system. None controls maritime law. Together, they commission joint scientific studies on pollution flows, submit coordinated evidence to international maritime organisations, and align local regulations with emerging standards. Over time, their data informs guidelines adopted by flag states. The tide line shifts. What began as local management becomes regional norm-setting.

The motif here is *the tide line*. It marks where land meets sea, where authority blurs. Microstates operate along such lines. So do cities and non-state actors. Those who learn to read the tide line anticipate change rather than react to it.

A limitation deserves attention. Not all microstate tactics translate cleanly. Sovereign states benefit from legal standing that others lack. Access can be withdrawn. Coalitions can fracture. Non-state actors risk being dismissed as advocates rather than partners. The reconciliation lies in realism. Adaptation includes recognising when formal authority is indispensable and when informal influence suffices.

Observable behaviours distinguish effective adaptation from naïve imitation. Successful actors invest in institutional memory, even without permanent missions. They document interactions, maintain contact lists, and track procedural calendars. They speak the language of the forum, avoiding slogans. They accept incremental gains. These behaviours mirror those of experienced small-state diplomats.

Metrics again matter. For cities, influence may be measured by references to their standards in national legislation. For indigenous organisations, by the inclusion of their knowledge in official reports. For firms, by early consultation invitations. These indicators guide strategy. They also discipline ambition.

A second named example sharpens the point. The Global Covenant of Mayors for Climate and Energy, formalised in 2016 in Brussels, coordinated thousands of cities around emissions reporting and targets. By standardising data, the network increased its credibility with financial institutions and national governments. The technique echoed microstate leverage: turn technical compliance into bargaining power. The consequence was access to funding streams previously reserved for states.

Still, caution is warranted. Over-coordination can dull responsiveness. Networks may prioritise consensus over effectiveness. Microstates face the same tension. The solution is selective alignment. Actors choose when to speak collectively and when to act alone. This judgement improves with experience.

The broader implication is unsettling for traditional diplomacy. Influence no longer belongs exclusively to those with flags. It accrues to those who understand process, timing, and narrative. Microstates learned this out of necessity. Others can learn it by choice.

The tide line returns at the close of this section. As global governance fragments, more actors find themselves operating at the edge of formal authority. They can retreat, or they can study how microstates turned constraint into craft. The test is not whether they resemble states, but whether they read the currents accurately.

The sharpened choice is clear. Adapt proven diplomatic practices to new contexts, accepting limits while exploiting openings, or cling to outdated models that assume power flows only from size and status. The lessons are available. The question is who will apply them with discipline.

About the Author

Selma Aarvik writes about the quiet edges of world politics, where island capitals and small city states negotiate with far larger powers. Her work follows the people who stand at microphones, in courtrooms and in corridors on behalf of countries that most atlases barely name. She is especially interested in how climate vulnerability, maritime law and public finance collide in the lives of real officials. Growing up on a northern coastline where weather, ferries and fishing seasons shaped daily life, she learned early how much distant decisions affect small communities. That memory runs through her writing on microstates, globalisation and ocean governance. Over the years she has written essays, briefings and longform profiles that make abstruse institutions and treaties legible to general readers. Her guiding aim is to show how seemingly minor offices and meetings quietly redirect trade, money and emissions. Rather than treating diplomacy as an elite game, she focuses on patient craft, institutional memory and the stories envoys tell at home when the conferences end. In this book she brings together years of close listening to diplomats, lawyers and organisers from small states to show how they manage to move cargo, climate and capital with very limited hard power.

www.ingramcontent.com/pod-product-compliance
Lightning Source LLC
Chambersburg PA
CBHW031337230926
51848CB00002B/274
9789376556823